Where We Find Ourselves

Poems and Stories
of Maps and Mapping
from

UK Writers of the Global Majority

Edited by
Sandra A Agard and Laila Sumpton

ARACHNE PRESS

First published in UK 2021 by Arachne Press Limited
100 Grierson Road, London SE23 1NX
www.arachnepress.com
© Arachne Press 2021
ISBNs
Print 978-1-913665-44-9
eBook 978-1-913665-45-6
Audio 978-1-913665-47-0

Thanks to Muireann Grealy for her proofing.
Thanks to Komal Madar for her cover design.
Printed on wood-free paper in the UK by TJ Books, Padstow.

The publication of this book is supported using public funding by the National Lottery through Arts Council England.

Acknowledgements

A Glossary of Terms © Sami Ibrahim 2021

A Man's Space © Mallika Khan 2021

A Place to Call © Sandra Nimako-Boatey 2021

A ship on the horizon doesn't make me feel less alone and *The Selden Map* © L Kiew 2021

A Walk in the Countryside © Dipika Mummery 2021

Anchusa and *East Coast* © Yvie Holder 2021

Anvils and Canals © Farhana Khalique 2021

Baseline Measurements © Anita Goveas 2021

Biafra © Catherine Okoronkwo 2021

Capillary Motion and *Hi-Spy Viewing Machine* © Rachael Li Ming Chong 2021

Cocoon Lucky © Kavita A. Jindal 2021

Colourful Chart © Meng Qiu 2021

Departure Lounge © Rhiya Pau 2021

Geography Lesson and *They Call Themselves Las Águilas Del Desierto / Eagles of the Desert* © Marina Sánchez 2021

Haibun for Your Return and *Translate This Sentence* © Dean Atta 2021

Ife and *The Mother I Never Met* © PA Bitez 2021

Invasion © Crystal Koo 2021

Jallianwalla Bagh © Nikita Aashi Chadha 2021

Journey to the Land Unknown © Mimi Yusuf 2021

Make Me Into a River and *To Hope* © ZR Ghani 2021

Managing Through a Pandemic: Hands Face Space © Lorraine Mighty 2021

Mermaid Visits the Archive © Gita Ralleigh 2021

My Fault © Marka Rifat 2021

My Sister's Care Home Promises © Shamini Sriskandarajah 2021

Repatriation © Selina Nwulu 2021

Rollercoasters and *We Painted the Sky* © Ambrose Musiyiwa 2021

Running on the Spot © Des Mannay 2021

Runway Flower © Désirée Reynolds 2021

SE16 © Oluwaseun Olayiwola 2021

Silver Line © Savannah Sevenzo 2021

Speak Me a Poem © Emily Abdeni-Holman 2021

Where We
Find Ourselves

Contents

Introduction
Sandra A Agard and Laila Sumpton

Where We Find Ourselves is an anthology of poetry and short stories that will take you on a journey from Beirut to Columbo, Port of Spain to the US/Mexican border and then to the Atlantic floor. You'll travel to the Black Mother's Yoga class, soar with a kite over Victoria Park and sail with Dutch colonial ships to China.

You'll navigate past worlds, possible worlds, mythologies and memories from the writers, new and established, who responded to our theme of *maps and mapping.*

You will encounter poems and stories that investigate where we find home, identities lost and found, colonial history, exile, family and much more. where would your travels take you if you were to map your journey?

This is a book that celebrates global majority writers, and our authors self-identify in many ways: African, African American, Arab, Asian, Bangladeshi, Black, Black British, Black British Caribbean, Black African, British Asian, British African Caribbean, British Indian, British Lebanese, British Sri Lankan, British Pakistani, Caribbean, Chinese, Chinese-Filipino, Chinese-Malaysian, Indian, Indigenous Mexican Latinx, Human, Middle Eastern, Mixed Race, South Asian, and Tamil. Our anthology gives a platform to rich and varied voices, many of whom have been marginalised in the publishing world.

The need for publishing more global majority writers became

clearer and more urgent when the Black Lives Matter movement was given a renewed global focus following the murder of George Floyd at the hands of US police in May 2020. It is important that diverse stories and histories are told by writers of that heritage, so that future generations can see themselves in the books they read, and understand who they are.

Even the subtitle of our book, *Poems and Stories of Maps and Mapping from UK Writers of the Global Majority*, is at the heart of the UK's race identity debates. Definitions are constantly changing and until there is more equality, spaces for diverse writers need to be supported with open discussion and without recrimination.

We hope you enjoy your voyage, and arrive at many unexpected places in *Where We Find Ourselves*.

Be Manzini
Survival Protocol

In the case of Mercator vs
Truth, Mercator is victorious
and Africa is forced
to squeeze into Europe.
So I'm mapping out my body
in a shape the
privileged can
understand.

Femininity is unallowed
in this version, there are no
hills or mountains to
conquer.
So much safer; flat,
plain,
less likely to be
colonised if I cover
me in snow.

Does anything natural
and rich grow in blind whiteness?

I yearn to uncover the
soil of my skin, the
peaks of me,
the tributaries between legs... my
lips in full bloom... my
hair... untouched long grass.
Smoke screen... thick...
Frozen... I can breathe.

They touch me, consent
ungiven, fold away when they
are done. Stolen continent
stowed in ships and chests then
tossed in a bottom privy
chamber in Gerardus'
fourteenth century stony castle.

I still can't fathom
how we got here.

ZR Ghani
Make Me Into a River

Chaos seeks an uninhabitable home.

A light held on my tongue
of words unspoken
is the signal fire.

Give yourself fear, give yourself doubt
to channel your way into my shoes.

There are seasons in me
which do not reflect the Earth's.
Each tide drowns me a little
and moves on – that's life,
sweeping up oaks, washing
away the road that leads to peace.

Rivers aren't lost so I'll be the first,
sifting ashes from stardust;
birds fly though damaged wings
while I resign, with the same surrender
that hot glass drinks air, into tributaries
that run screeching, untethered,
scribbling out a drought.

A pain contorting all of time.
So this is how love takes root.

L Kiew
The Selden Map

A map is the opposite of floating
on water attached to nothing.
Sanyapi bears care and hope,
Quanzhou merchants, small boats
ducking the Dutch blockade.

The British with their free trade
are only smoke blown over,
a brief turn in the shade and
old ways guided by new light.
Water slaps time against sides.

Scent of poppy sap and no one
moves further up the line.
Today I smell of sandalwood,
look for needlepaths, sequence
bearings from home ports.

*The Selden Map has been held in the Bodleian Library since 1659. It was
rediscovered in 2008.
Historians have traditionally argued that East Asia, as a whole, had no
indigenous cartography.*

Rachael Li Ming Chong
Capillary Motion

My ancestors peeped over a pyramid of freckled pears,
through smoke ribbons of agarwood to witness
my graduation to words with more permanence.

No more pencil – a fountain pen, gifted from the family shop;
they *gānbēied* raucously at the promise tint in its trail,
Roman letters scrawled over borders Ah Tai Kong never

crossed. It came with a bottle of Quink, souped up with sweat
wrung from Po Po's neck towel and sirens circled
along the glass rim. They shook it wildly to infuriate the ink.

It fermented tartly in its cartridge and surged out
across paper lines, brittle boned *hanzi* skittling
in its wake: *won't, can't, shouldn't, couldn't; pierce, piece,*

priest, belief; knock, knee, knowledge, knife;
a continuous line of cursive trans-continental ghosts
would tug upon, nodding as it held its place.

In science class I unscrewed the bottom shell to marvel
at its reservoir glow in front of the fluorescent fixtures.
I learned how to lemon-soak my words without applying heat.

The split of the nib – it grew tired, warped ink
to a manuscript of blots increasingly only I could decipher.
See now my hands, they linger. Waiting,

for the gasp before the mark, the flow of liquid into narrow spaces.

Amanda Addison
The Hand You Were Dealt Before You Were Born

He could have shaken my hand in welcome on arrival at Newark Airport. After all, I had crossed half the globe, spent hours nose stuck to the triple-glazed glass – gazing out through the round window. Spread out below: a patchwork of Arctic white and cool blues. The kittiwake's view.

And in that semi-comatose state of the long-haul traveller, I remembered a film: *The Island on Top of the World.* Foolhardy explorers circumnavigated by hot air balloon, frostbitten fingers, and toes. I pulled the thin complimentary blanket tightly around my shoulders.

The lighting was not kind in Arrivals. He looked on suspiciously. At the head of the queue a man with a cane hobbled along. The police dog came, sniffed the walking stick and he was through!

My turn. He asked me to lay my hand upon the scanner. He mapped my past, my present, my future. His hand had a horseshoe tattoo. He took an imprint. A copy. A facsimile. That ancient mark declared: *She is here! She has arrived!*

He had a simulacrum of me, meanwhile the real me was on the loose, crossed 32nd Street, marvelled at the steam clouds rising up – vapour plumes, falling fountains on the sidewalk – matchstick people, wrapped up warm in black and grey, barged past.

Lonely in the spacious sanctuary of my hotel room for two, I turned the television on. News anchors beamed into my room from the other side of this enormous land. They stood in front of palm trees and swimming pools as if posing for a Hockney.

15

Was the border guard staring intently at our handprints? Always superstitious, with his lucky horseshoe tattoo. Could he read my heart line, head line, life line? My Mount of Venus?

His Irish forebears measured horses in hands. His Norwegian ancestors used a 'thumb', a carpenter's measure – banged Thor's hammer to build a pioneer's house, where quilts were carefully stitched by the hand which rocked the cradle.

A kindergarten group enter Battery Park. Hands linked like paper-chain people. A vision in Technicolor! The willow charcoal sticks of trees look on. The children spy a row of miniature wooden houses – beehives on stilts, painted in pastels.

Will they return to class and play once again with the doll's house? Such busy bees? Or maybe they'll make handprints, forever small on their Mother's Day cards.

My phone vibrates. I cradle it in my palm. A fingerprint unlocks me and reveals a message, from my daughter: just landed. I turn on my heels and head out of the park.

Meng Qiu
Colourful Chart

When I was a child
I studied the map on my wall
finding myself in a grey town
surrounded by black lines, separated.

Beyond those borders, I heard people cry,
I tried to communicate but nobody understood.

So, I picked up my brush and began to depict
with strokes of fate running through my mind
colours burst into middle of the night.

In this vibrancy all boundaries disappeared
and while hueing the world, I felt safe.

Later I looked at the map again
limits of division had diminished.

I saw families walk, hand in hand
dancing, laughing and over their heads
a beautiful rainbow appeared
staining my dreams in abundance.

L Kiew
A ship on the horizon doesn't make me feel less alone

Why are you making my skin a map?
Do you think a map gives you
the right to tour and traverse
each tender point, tidal plunge
and storm between archipelagos?

What are you drawing on the map?
Where do you think you're putting your X?
Do you think your tongue welcome
trading along isthmus and isle?
You think your map will help me

find the way. Your voice in my ear –
closer than I accept – is unwelcome.
I refute your missionary
position, its overgrown bone pile.
Do you think I don't know how?

Lorraine Mighty
Managing Through a Pandemic: Hands – Face – Space

These hands	This face	That space
Guide	Smiles	Consumed
Support	Provides	With trauma
Sustain	Gentle	Unheard
Comfort	Reassurance	Unnoticed

These hands	That face	That space
Reach out	Blank	Hollow
From home	But nods	Of care
To foster	To attest	Consequence
Belonging	It's listening	Compassion

Those hands	This face	This space
Dispatch	Pleads	A gulf
Commands	With hope	Between us
Compliant	In grief	Corroding
Complicit	Drowning	Connection

Selina Nwulu
Repatriation

Jimmy Aldaoud

was deported to Iraq and, upon dying sixty-three days later, is
returned and buried in U.S. soil.
His name, the trigger to a removal order, as keen and precise as
a bullet to the jugular.
A man picked up and dropped like a chess piece, proving
nothing but the game we've become
and this is war continuing. A bitter homecoming, allegiance to
the flag only in dying.

Jimmy finally an American, great again.

Benson Egwuonwu
The Lie

cast your hand
over this parchment of land
and dream deep the means to seize it for I,

engineer the weapons
to expel the residents
or erect the catechism to ensure they comply,

pillage their property
their markets and libraries
and bury any rebellion in a mass shallow grave,

then

tuck away your gun
while you lick your silver tongue
and swear there was no civilization when you came.

Marina Sánchez
Geography Lesson

The tall, white, blue-eyed PE teacher,
stands in front of the Year 9 class.
                              I am supporting students.
The topic: Colonising America.
Thanks to watching Pocahontas,
most recognise the map of Virginia.
Why did they go there?
No answers. He goes on:
Because there was no one there.
He repeats:
Because there was no one there.
Smiling, he adds:
Vast expanses of land and wealth to exploit,
perfect for making a fortune.
Some students take notes.
                    I cannot speak for the explosive
                    element in my bones, blood, breath.

         It doesn't matter what I did *afterwards*.

                    Like asking if he realised
         he'd wiped out my ancestors in his class.
                              He didn't reply.
                    Didn't speak to me for months.

My silence has been flensing me since then.

Crystal Koo
Invasion

On a red-fingered morning, the ritual begins. The waters recede with a slow sucking noise, the shore rises like a spectre and meets the mountaintop. The trees fall, breaking at the belly, littering the newly made hillside with grey bodies splotched with lichen and fungus. The land splits into canyons, cratering into new valleys. Cliffs fall and the hills jerk away into parcels of earth, forming land bridges. Like clockwork, the frost of winter arrives, looking to colonise the edges of what has broken apart. Slender, silvery fish jostle into ridges flooded with water. The birds have long gone.

A few families are present on a rocky strip of beachfront. They stand around bundled in blankets and heavy clothing, bags on their backs. Waves lap the shore, an overlooked patch of calm. Someone kicks a rock. No one lights a fire.

At another beachfront, unluckier families are swept away by the returning waters. The ones who hid in the forest have been swallowed into the dark, earthy maw, joining the deer and the foxes.

Many people have fled on boats to other lands, where they have bought houses. They watch their own land rearrange itself from afar. They had watched their hired soldiers mow down people who had tried to take their boats once the first tremors of the ritual had been felt. The exiles had planned their survival, sacrificed time that could have been spent singing and dancing in festivals to secure boats, houses, permits. No one had the right to take these away from them.

In the city, everything is louder. The buildings shatter, first the glass then the keening of steel. The highways point their jagged pieces of concrete to the sky, cars clinging to them like desperate parasites on a great fish. Schools pour out furniture. Temples plunge into the belly of the earth, the roads break into black, dusty wafers. Utility poles tangle until they snap in sparks and fire. The sewers flood.

Then it settles.

Survivors shuffle out to see their new world. They have come from the hilltops. Or the caves, which they had prayed were deep enough to be taken whole when the earth moved. Outside, new roads have been made, indentations on the earth paved with rubble. The trees that have survived bend toward the sun in a different angle. Old cliffs that were once phantoms in the fog now appear in the middle of the city, like new gods. Hills have been hewn into slabs, crammed with fossils and graves, and fused into new combinations.

The people bury the dead they can find. They start rebuilding. Their fences gone; they fight about property. They talk of everything but how their old stories float in the air with nowhere to attach themselves. Where is the theatre with the strange, indecipherable movie last week? The hospital that caught fire? There is too much work to be done. There will be new tides to the rivers, new locations for mudslide and quicksand.

The ones who had boats – do they return? Unlikely, unless they are on their deathbeds and their minds are free. For now they turn away, sorrowful and repulsed. What makes people want to rebuild, to only be reduced to debris in another twenty-five years? In their guilt, they whisper about the stubbornness and the misguided loyalty of the ones who stay. The exiles wander in their new homes, buying new salt and pepper shakers, while their homeland throbs like a wound far away.

The ones who stay send up balloons to learn the heights of their new mountains.

The gods of the land had been carefree and content. They made liquor from sweet tree sap, played bead games, wooed each other with guitars. They were indifferent to the people, who lived at a polite distance from them. The trees rained fruit. The earth was unmoved.

Then other gods came. Gods from seas away, gigantic and fiery-haired, faces craggy like demons, their ears glowing in the hot sun. Intrigued, the gods of the land offered them sweet tree sap. These other gods spun golden words, danced around the gods of the land, plied them with poppy juice.

Dawn found the gods of the land beheaded in their sleep and the land transformed by the new gods. The waterways and the mountains had not been to their liking, not what it was like at home. The new gods had felt compelled to righten the map. They had broken the mountains into pieces, hurling sacks of earth across the land. Sinkholes yawed. The new gods rerouted the waters. This was the first ritual.

The new gods made temples for themselves that the people were not to enter. The people pained them. Their strange language, the fear for their lives. The people clamoured for their dead and their ravaged land. The new gods were unimpressed. The trees sap had dried up because the new gods were always thirsty. They grew restless and looked to the sea once more.

The new gods gave the people a final gift before they left. The new gods broke off parts of themselves and shattered them into small pieces, lodging themselves into the people's eyes so they would always know how to remake their land in the gods' image.

Through the splinters, the people saw themselves as the new gods had seen them: irrelevant, inadequate, lacking. Every twenty-five years the splinters came together on one red-fingered morning, not unlike the morning the new gods came, and the ritual began anew.

The ones who escaped on boats carry the pieces of the gods

in their eyes. In their new homes, the people around them also speak like those gods, the greengrocer's ears glow in the sun. The exiles trip over the words of their new language and their ears do not glow. They are always surrounded by whispers, words like spun gold, and they do not understand their intention.

The years pass. The exiles are better at the language, although everyone else still find their food too pungent, too complicated. The exiles don't know what to say about this. They buy less exciting food. Perhaps if they do this, they will become more than mechanics and nurses. They buy a big television. When they meet a stranger whom they can tell has come from home (consciously well-dressed, loud in their enjoyment but quiet when spoken to), they avoid each other. From afar, their homeland turns itself inside out. The exiles sigh and turn the television off. Too much news is bad for mental health. When relatives come to visit, the exiles proudly give them local sweets as gifts to take home. They talk to their relatives in their new language, their effort to mimic the accent correctly slowing them down. They bring their guests to see their new television, riveted to a wall that will never fall. The shards in everyone's eyes glow. The exiles feel better.

The visitors return home, to houses that never feel solid despite how deep the concrete is poured into the earth. They make tea and gulp down the sweets their relatives have given them. They put the radio on and watch the birds return. They make exciting food. Secretly they wonder if their relatives, in their new place, pity them. It will be another few years before the next remaking. Sometimes they think of the last painful movement of the final remaking and wonder if they will live through it. They think of other lands. They think of how their tongues will never straighten to mimic new accents correctly, but their children might. Their eyes itch. They rub them, tired from the journey.

Nikita Aashi Chadha
Jallianwalla Bagh

all you can see
are the bullet holes
pretty pennies decorate the bottom of a well
they carry the wishes of the slain

flowers bloom
strangers smile
they mask the reality
the brutality
the spilling of innocent blood

the flashbacks
come hard and fast
I can see the narrow passages
I can't move
I can't breathe
the bodies are piling

won't you stop and take a selfie with me?

when did places of tragedy
start taking bookings for vanity?
when did landmarks start to mark our downfall?

PA Bitez
The Mother I Never Met

grief is the taste on my tongue when
africa reaches her hand out to me
and i have nothing to say to her

i do not speak the same language as my mother /
she speaks / & i cannot speak back /
i did not inherit the silk / the gold / the fat – of that continent /

i never met one of her sisters or experienced
the softness of their opened hands / under the gaze of Europe
i am a daughter with no motherland /

for people who can't leave their skin
or hair behind when asked about origins
we cry

i was persuaded out of my own skin /
my own language / my own mind

did anyone tell you that pain is a mouth? /
how it eats you

i am full on all things visceral /
the richest place on earth is my mother's house /
except for her own people /

africa hands her guests
petals yet she is greeted with pistols /

and i have nothing to her
because she speaks & i cannot speak back /
i did not inherit the silk / the gold / the fat – of that continent.

Catherine Okoronkwo
Biafra

I
Papa told me about civil war on Nigerian soil. Years
of ethnic turmoil boiled over, until knives and cutlasses hacked
dreams, scattered under polluted palm trees.

The slogans: 'secession', 'rejection of colonial mapping',
'freedom fighters'. Unforgotten moment, best forgotten?
Defining, for thousands of proud Igbos, like Papa,

left bleeding, battle-scarred, bitter. Suckling babies cried to
Chukwu, hidden from ghosts with full stomachs.
On every side, bullets and bombs. Hunger killed more.

Butchered, burned or abandoned, left for fattened rats to chew.
Ndi ala beke fell silent silent   silent.
The colonial enterprise had eyes on the prize, and dismembered
a nation, gouging her heart.

II

I brought an Efik boy home. Dark complexion, dimples. 'An Efik man is not an Igbo man,' my parents said.
I had dinner with a Yoruba man, stylish in luxurious agbada,

drenched in cologne. 'Never forget Biafra,' my parents said. An Hausa man was out of the question. No loved Igbo daughter could end up in the north. The compromise, a White man?

'Learn from them, never be bewitched,' my parents said. They spoke in unison, echoed each other. 'Never forget who you are and where you came from,' they said.

Emily Abdeni-Holman
Speak Me a Poem

The sky is dark now
and I have tried to light a candle
with a cigarette I smoke
for no purpose other than to watch waves
waft through dimming sky–

Connection to a place
depends on people, a fact
I have not felt so clearly as now
when fragility is sifting through night air
and Jamhour and Beirut light the misting dark.

Pine needles flicker in wind,
and lights marking nightfall and routine
tell of people living, on through a backdrop
of precarity, and insecurity, and a flu
that catches on, on, including you I love.

It is getting cold now.
Hot tea is comforting. And elsewhere,
a house nearby, things happening to you I love
cannot be known by me. Until a voicenote
arrives softly, saying, My fever is down. Speak a poem to me.

The request made me cry.
And I'm almost afraid to hear my voice
in the dark, pretending promise,
putting words to it across Lebanon's evening
to be played to your fever, before it rises.

For months I have felt guilt
until day begins to fade and night calls
itself forward, settling over all this–
Gates closing, food cooking, water warming.
And instead of saying your poem

I'm on my third cigarette,
waiting for my stomach to calm itself
enough for me to gather a voice
and speak someone else's words
into a phone, solitary, for you to hear.

There is no close to this.
We have been waiting, all this time,
and I see in the waiting a fear of life
so great that everything stops,
even poetry, in the new year's night–

Electricity goes, and with it my connection.
My voice in the night will be like
a promise to stability, when all of Lebanon is afraid, and me.
Yesterday was a woman's song, young woman
singing hope on a stairway.

Promises live mostly in hearts
and cannot often be felt.
I do not want to resist reality. I want only
to hold the sky to it, great dusk sky,
the fell of dark, and voice.

Farhana Khalique
Anvils and Canals

There's a giant anvil in Regent's Park. I think it is as surprised as we are that it is here, because it has fallen over. The flat end buried in the grass, the pointy bit aimed at heaven. As if dropped straight out of a cartoon sky. There's even an animal on it.

'That's my favourite,' says Laila.

I follow my best friend. Close up, the figure is balanced with one leg on the point, the other leg raised high, along with one arm. One ear is cocked like an antenna.

'That is so random,' I say, and Laila exchanges smiles with the metal hare. The whole structure is the colour of a shadow, though it doesn't cast much of one itself in the midday brightness. It's as smooth as a pebble, with a livid shine.

'I like the hare,' says Laila. 'It feels like he's about to take off.'

I look up at the gangly humanoid thing, but the clouds behind him are so pale it hurts. I turn away and blink back milky spots, pulling forward the peak of my hijab and hoping I don't get a migraine.

'Mariam?' Laila is watching me. 'Shall we move on?' she asks, and I nod.

When I'd asked if she wanted to catch up over lunch this Saturday, she'd suggested we make an adventure out of it. I hadn't seen her since she came back from South Korea, so I was going to suggest one of our old foodie favourites in Shepherd's Bush, maybe a bit of shopping. I'd even grabbed a *Time Out* and tossed it in my bag, thinking we would flick through it together, and make more plans. Then she told me about the sculpture exhibition in the park and a new vegan place she wanted to try, and asked me if I'd like to walk along Regent's Canal. So I said sure, and swapped my glasses for contacts and put on make-up and a flowery dress. Then Laila turned up in ripped jeans and grubby Converses and I almost laughed out loud.

Now, this is more like it, I think as we walk on and enter a rose garden, each leggy bloom like a supermodel that knows how to work the light. I like the red ones. They're as bold as lipstick, perfectly offset by waxy leaves held like hundreds of reflectors.

'This is gorgeous,' I say.

'Thought you'd like it,' says Laila, and I'm touched. She adds, 'Wish I'd discovered it sooner. Then again, we don't get that long for lunch.'

I try and picture her in the grand white building she pointed out before we entered the park. I was surprised when she told me she'd accepted a non-teaching job with such a stuffy old company, but then I'd figured she wanted a change after her two years at the international school. Now, I imagine her racing though her paperwork, then surfing the net and plotting her next holiday.

We continue through the park and come across a small bridge. It overlooks a floating restaurant and some smaller barges and we pause.

'I'd love to live on a boat,' says Laila, leaning over.

'Really?' I hover by her elbow, wondering if I've misheard.

'Yeah. Looked into it after I got back, thought it might be cheaper than buying a flat. Then I heard the council was trying to increase the mooring fees and god knows what else.' She shakes her head and her sunglasses flash.

'Scumbags,' I say, but still wondering if she's serious. 'You'd hate it in the winter, though.'

'True. That's what put me off.' She turns away.

We leave the bridge and step down to the water.

It is another world here, full of people and bicycles and dogs and more boats. Some of these are moored and some are not, and some are like floating vegetable gardens, bursting with cherry tomatoes and rhubarb and countless leaves drizzled in sunshine.

We continue walking and I tell her about my new classes at school, and she tells me about her new admin role. I've never worked in an office, but you would think Laila's forgotten what it is like being in a classroom already, in the space of a summer.

'Are you really leaving teaching?' I say.

'Well, this is only temporary, so who knows. But for now, yeah.'

'Oh.' It falls like a sigh, and Laila notices.

'Mariam, I'm surprised you've stayed this long! Hardly anyone else from our tutor group's still doing it.'

I recall our old PGCE crew, their last Facebook updates and pics. She's right. 'I can't imagine doing anything else,' I say, looking at the weeds.

'Oh you should.' She turns to me. 'If you want to,' she says, but she's got that look in her eye. The same one I saw when she was telling me about Korea and how I should join her. I'd said I wanted to stay and go for the Head of Year position, I could always travel later. Now though, she's practically bouncing. 'You know what, I'll let you know if I hear of anything interesting. The agency had tonnes of leads before I took this job.'

'Nah, that's alright,' I say. I don't know what's brighter; Laila's face, or the sun. She has forgotten I can't handle the heat. I should have tied my hijab up in a turban today. I should sit for a bit, find some shade, but I don't want to make a fuss.

'Do you have a CV?' says Laila. 'If not, I can help–'

'—No, really, I...' I trail off. At some point during the walk, we've entered another dimension.

The living traffic has thinned out and the path has widened. Aside from the occasional barge or merry GoBoat, there's just green-dappled water. On the far side, a sweep of weeping willows trail their tendrils. It's a glorious halo of an afternoon, but there are welcome clouds too. The light plays hide and seek, flickering on the silky surface.

'It doesn't feel like we're in London, does it?' says Laila, taking off her shades and propping them above her fringe.

I agree. It's like our own little pocket of quiet. Suddenly, I wish I'd made more of an effort to visit Laila while she was out in Seoul. But it was so hot there when the others went over last summer, and the flights were so expensive. And she could have gone anywhere if she just wanted to work abroad for a bit, why did she pick somewhere so far away? I could have tried harder, though... but what's the point of that thought now? I shake it away.

'Are you glad you're back?' I say, sneaking a glance at her.

'Yeah, it's nice seeing everyone again. The school wanted me to stay on for another two years though, it's good money. Said the offer's still open, to let them know by October.'

I shudder. *Don't do it. You've only just come back*, I want to say. But I don't.

We continue, passing the Zoo, and the high walls of the aviary lean over us. Huge wings beat against the grey mesh. *So, is this how it starts?* I think. Maybe she will go back, and stay another year, and another. What if she meets a guy out there? Or fancies another country? After all, Anisha moved to Dubai when she got married and we've already lost track of which kid has had what birthday. Cards will become texts, and then belated ones. Weeks and months will concertina out, till we are no longer in tune.

The next bridge we come to is more grand, with sandy coloured sides and huge pillars with deep grooves. These are a dark olive colour and cool to the touch, as I stop and stand in their purpley shade. I turn to Laila. *Don't do it.* It's on my tongue. *Don't do it, don't do it, don't do it.* 'Laila?'

'Yep?'

'I... We should do this more often.'

She's by the next pillar and for a second she looks confused. Then she beams. 'Of course. I'll look up more random walks.' She comes back.

I smile too, relieved. 'And I'll look up more random restaurants.'

Laila laughs. 'Speaking of which – I'm starving. We can get back up to street level from here.'

We go, leaving the water shushing the banks, like a lullaby, or a goodbye.

Gita Ralleigh
Mermaid Visits the Archive

By the shore, she remembers
once diving the wreck.

Though they told her never
to adventure its depths

or harvest its bones, cast
as oracle on ocean floor.

She witnessed a rotten hull
give way, from tarry gloom

the dull gleam of mercury,
copper ingots' cold clink.

She longs to recall the stink
of death. No documents

but papered dissolution.
She seeks herself in ivory

and iron, salt-cured skins
elephant tusks, stone shot,

fragments of pelvis. Later
she learns to hide her tail

beneath long skirts. Land-
dweller, she gathers a form

from museum dust. Between
mammoth and meteorite she

reads of affinity with elephants,
her twin pairs of breasts–how

when strapped to a mast, she
gains ecstasies–a voice pitched

to scream, which some sailors
call her song. She feels the stone

weighting her chest. Ghosts of
coins spill silver from her mouth.

Lorraine Dixon
The Leaving

Dedicated to Grace Nichols and Joan Riley and other black writers of poetry and prose who weave marginalised narratives into the warp and weft of British (his)story.

I am not a long memoried
woman like Grace.
My memories are few
and far between
                              lost
in the dust of trauma
in the lick of pain
her pain
his pain
our pain
We don't speak of it
They choose silence
to hide the shame
to ignore the ache
to forget the leaving of the
big island. Their children's
names are 'mystery upon mystery',
'never got to know them'
and 'missed opportunities'.

Joan understands all of this,
the regrets
the long goodbyes
the legacy of separations
chasing ol' massa's dreams
whilst their old families
are left behind.
New children grow up fast
in the Motherland
forever stranger to the heart's home
severed from those rooted there.

Rhiya Pau
Departure Lounge

In memory of our elders who lost their lives to Coronavirus in London's care homes.

In those days, your loved ones could see you off
from the runways. You see them shrinking fast,
holding on to promises, suddenly indistinguishable –
to call, to write, to send money, holding on to the land
you call home while you rattle through the air in a tin plane,
hollow as the cola cans boys kick down the dirt tracks,
sweat glistening on the black muscle of their backs.

No welcome party at Heathrow, only long looks
at your tea-stained skin, arm hairs raised, nine yards
not enough to keep your body from shaking. Holding on
to a suitcase of wool and *murtis*, incense and coconut shell,
red *tilak* to anoint your new home. Outside, the air is cold
and dry and you think to yourself: *How can this be
the same star-studded night that blinds the Serengeti?*

Through the seventies, planes flock from Bwindi
and the Masai Mara, migrating bloodlines of Saurashtra,
reconvene in London. Depart: bilingual with clammy palms
and first-flier nerves. Arrive: tongue-tied, mouths filled
with broken glass, shards of English. No welcome party
at Heathrow. But you feed them *rotli-shak*, let them stay,
two-by-two for a few days in your one bed on Greenford High
Road, sprawled on plastic sofas, battling the heavy-headedness
that comes only from taking leaps so big, they cross oceans.

You will share a home with them again, in your eighties,
when you are widowed. And in that home, where they serve
rotli-shak, open the morning with incense and *bhajan*,
a generation is fed and washed by the same hands, a chorus
of stories tells a history of the gold they buried in Jinja,
ruthless dictators, fickle empire, first flier nerves, brown
woollen jumpers of immigrant Britain. In days, eight decades
are quietly erased, a breathless chorus grieving for those days,
when your loved ones could see you off from the runways.

Ngoma Bishop
The Inner City Kite that Yearns for Freedom

What a spectacular, wondrous, awesome sight
Yuh West Indian Singing Kite
Yuh humming, zinging, singing kite yuh
Yuh rising and dipping kite yuh
Watch how yuh just climbing and diving doe
Striving to escape duh captivity of dat string
On yuh broad nose
Damn string seeking to keep yuh under even closer control
To temper yuh very soul

Look how yuh does soar doe
Higher ever higher
Yuh wondrous potential high flyer yuh

Fly kite fly
Display yuh kaleidoscope of colour
Across duh panoramic scope

Yuh black and red and gold and shades of green
So serene
Maybe duh most beautiful kite ever seen
Over Clissold, Springfield, Hackney Downs or Victoria Park
Prescribe yuh mathematically perfect and wondrous arc
Over Hackney and beyond

Raise yuh voice in a song of joy and hope
Sing yuh song, do
Yuh sweet, sweet ancestral zinging song
Sweeter even than yuh namesake kite or da cuckoo or da lark

Yet still yuh song of pain and sorrow
Of yesterdays, today and tomorrows
Reminiscent of tales and times not to be forgotten
Stories still unfolding
Ever unfolding
Mimicking muh dreams and memories
Wid yuh tail flowing proudly behind yuh
For duh children too must soar
Likewise duh grandchildren

So bruk free kite, bruk free now
Sail free over duh little river Lea
Towards duh Caribbean Sea
Bruk free kite
Bruk free and mek muh smile again
Bruk free
Bruk free nuh
Bruk free

Désirée Reynolds
Runway Flower

The sky had always covered her, her whole life, all day from one morning to the next. It covered her, her family and school, the sea, it covered her Grandada's mountain, all the way over to the next parish. She never knew if at some point the sky just stopped, it never let her find out because it always followed wherever she went.

*

She looked with big hunting eyes, tired, fighting to keep them open at her new home. Ribbon flapped around her head, like big ears searching. Florence clutched Miss P's hand. Miss P was coming to see her husband, stories reaching her back home of his outside family. She would always feel new here, she would always be waiting to get back on that plane.

'Now I want fi know is where you moder deh?'

Florence knew it was not a question, she had had thirteen hours of it. When people said it was unlucky for some she thought, not for her. Now she realised thirteen's unluckiness had caught up with her. She would always hate it. People moved without seeing her or Miss P, they passed straight over them and moved through them. The wind blew across the tarmac. Everyone from somewhere else slowly walked towards the building, its flags blowing in the greyness. It was the biggest building she had ever seen. White people pushed her and Miss P to get into the warm, she had never seen so many.

*

She had been sent for to repair her parents already broken marriage. It wouldn't work.

They had found her, in the rain, the night she found out she was going to England. She had heard about it many times. It was where her mother lived, it was where her father worked, money would come from there in small pale blue envelopes. But she didn't want to leave. What would she eat? What would she do? Did they know her? Maybe she could go, just to see the place an then come back tomorrow. She climbed the old cotton tree, older than the land that rooted it, the tree that shrank as she got older and found her spot, wood made smooth by her skin's connection to it, and laid down. Legs swinging, arms behind her head this was her favourite place. Here, she and the sky would chat, catch up, make each other laugh. Now as she walked down those too high steps from the plane, she looked up and almost cried out loud.

What was wrong with this sky, unwashed, grey, moving too slowly.

Where was her sky?

She had seen dark skies before, when it was about to push out its rain, it would go darker blue, grey-blue and before the birth of a storm, green. And when the storm was done, it hung, turned itself over and became her friend again. She didn't recognise this sky's face at all.

'What is wrong wid you, come on, you want di plane to tek we back?'

She stood on the runway, unclean, she and the other runway flowers that had poured out the plane, blooming amongst the concrete. They brought colour, loud laughter and ribbons. They all shivered.

Every step she imagined her Grandada and Aunty Cyn would run up to her, laughing, smiling, chatting, that this was all a joke and they hadn't meant to frighten her, that Miss P could go now, and find her own wayward husband, that they wanted their child back. It was all such a mistake and a 'come mek we get di nex plane home'.

Goosebump bumpies rose all over her. She only ever felt that way when she had to get the switch. Here she would have to get the belt, the iron flex, the coat hanger, broom handle… here in England, the goose bumps would be permanent. And no amount of coconut oil would help.

'She betta hurry up, beca me have to catch di bus.'

Nothing moved, not the sky, not the ground, not the faces. She and her fellow travellers started to walk towards the airport buildings.

*

The woman in uniform, with hair the colour of sugar cane and eyes the colour of soapy water in a wash basin, smiled at them.

'Are you alright?'

'Yes tank you.' Miss P's grip tightened.

'Do you need assistance?'

'No.'

The woman bent down and patted the little girl on the head. Her hand tangling briefly with the ribbon.

'Take care, sweetheart. You people are so beautiful.'

She walked away, turned and waved into the crowd. Women with eyes like cats and men in new suits wallowed her up. They pushed, shouted, held up papers with names on. There to welcome family they had never heard of, there to marry strangers, there to become parents again.

The ribbons watched, the little girl's face was shiny with cream.

'What is wrong wid dat woman, she no leave us di whole journey. Is why she want to talk to you?'

'Beca I keep her secret.'

'Wha? Is what you seh? What secret? Cho! Jus come on.'

Breathing in real air made her dizzy. She never wanted to go back on a plane ever. Life was too small in there.

*

When, as a teenager, she remembered what she had seen on the plane, it would make her cry, but as an adult, it would make her smile.

*

'What is it, why you can't keep still? Why me mus be trap wid you inna dis ting, me no know. You momma no have no money to come fi you herself.' And on went Miss P. Everyone called her Miss even though she had been married for many, many years. It was as if no one really acknowledged it, least of all Mr P.

'Me wan go pee pee.'

'Git up an gwan no, you no see di lady tell you where fi go!'

So she rocked along, she could hear herself sucking the sweet given to her by Grandada. She had kept it in her hands all this time, till child sweat made it sticky, she had intended to keep it forever. She was sure Miss P would've made her throw it away, so she put it in her mouth for safe keeping. In this way, she told herself, if she ate it, it would always be with her, Grandada would be in her insides.

*

Florence walked to the toilet. She stood outside, not knowing if it was free but too scared to ask. She could hear noises, grunting, giggles.

'Ssh, hush you lip no gyal.'

She could see through a tiny crack. She couldn't help it. Without thought or shame, she pressed herself against it and pressed her eyeball against the crack. All she could see was an ankle, pale pink tights swung from it like a snakeskin and a black shiny shoe that tapped the wall. She could see shapes, colours in the shiny shoes. Just like Grandada had taught her how shoes should look. The shoe kept gently tapped the wall. She manoeuvred round so she could see more. She tried to guess what the shapes were.

'Excuse me little girl, are you lost?' She jumped. A man like no other she had ever seen before smiled down at her. White, but brown, tall but hunched over, strong and yet weak looking. The tapping stopped.

'Waiting for the loo?'

'I want to pee pee.'

'Oh, er, ah, yes,' he walked away, nothing left for him to say. Had he been watching them too?

'Oh, hello,' her hair was newly fixed, her cheeks red, a shiny film of sweat covered her face.

'This toilet is occupied; I'll take you to the other one.'

She didn't see the man, she let herself be led.

*

'I want to pee pee.'

'Again, Jesus Christ on di cross you coulda tes' Job. Is how you love a pee pee so? Git up den no, an hurry up.'

It had been hours since she gone before. She jumped up, not wanting to hear any more of Miss P's argument. She rushed back to the same toilet, she stepped up as if stalking a prey like when she and cousin Stevie would try an catch bullfrogs in Grandada's trees, but it was empty. She looked around in there, she didn't really know what for, she wanted to know who the Island man was. She came out and had forgotten to use it.

The plane lurched forward, and she fell onto the lap of a man she would dream about forever.

'Whoa dere, you alright?'

She looked up into the prettiest teeth she ever saw, in the head of a man she had never seen. He was the colour of the world before dawn.

'What is di matter wid you, you shock?'

'No. You have pretty teet.'

'Well, tank you, Miss Forward.'

He laughed, threw back his head and let out home sound.

'Are you alright, sir?' the woman with cane-coloured hair stopped with a tray.

'Yes, tank you.'

She smiled a twitchy half smile and turned towards him, straightened her back, pushed out her small chest. Florence stood between them, looking at one then the other. She wanted to take the words that were left hanging and wrap them around both their necks. She looked down at all their shoes. Hers were shiny. He ran his tongue over his top, pretty teeth and slowly sucked.

'Bwoy, me tink me goin to like Hingland, wha you tink?' He turned to Florence, including her in the game.

She said the first thing that popped into her head, 'But will Hingland like you?'

'Ha! Bombo,' he laughed, digging his friend next to him in the ribs. 'Well, we goin see, Miss Forward, we goin see.'

'Come on little girl, I'll take you to the toilet.' She balanced her tray in the other hand so she could hold Florence's. She led her away, briefly turning back to see him strap himself in.

'Now you will keep our secret, won't you?' she asked as they walked.

Florence wasn't listening. She passed the other children, already crying, children already lost, children on their own, some were even younger than her. When Florence became a social worker, she would marvel at the ease in which people left their children. There was no thought at the nonchalant way that they were sent across the planet with strangers for company. There was no thought for the small bundles of need that only grew inside them as time went on. Children that she would go to school with, would share a ward with, children who would end up as her clients. She looked into their faces now, all those flowers, yet to bloom.

'Ok? This one's free. I'll come back for you.'

In the toilet, she thought about pretty teet and the woman with the cane-coloured hair and her barely remembered parents and she wanted to cry. All alone in the sky.

Back in her seat the runway came up to meet her. In the airport she reached up and took the hand of the woman who said she was her mother. As Florence was being pulled through people's legs, coats, and suitcases, she turned to see pretty teet salute her. She wanted to salute back. Cane hair passed them both without saying a word and his smile faded back to home. Outside under the unrecognisable sky Florence looked up and decided that this sky wasn't worth talking to.

Ambrose Musiyiwa
We Painted the Sky

1
the song was a bird
and it lived in the jungle
and it woke up each morning
and sang sleep off

the jungle was a story

the story was a hunger

2
we painted the sky,
populated it
   with fools about to step off precipices,
       month-long parties,
       trails of journeys taken,
       and possibilities

3
there was music in your voice

4
we iced the future with hope
and cast it across the sky
like stars

5
the hunger was like an ulcer
feeding on itself

Des Mannay
Running On The Spot

You're on a conveyor belt –
journey assured.
Occasionally it
judders to a halt –
some may fall off.

We are on the treadmill –
one trip, one slip,
one misunderstanding,
we go straight to hell.

Do not pass go.
Do not collect £200.
Stop and search: incarcerate.
Swell prison's population.

Murderers march streets
dressed in black –
'protect and swerve'
this is the justice they dispatch.

Victims' last cry?
For the mother –
those who birth us but
are not there at the end.

From the cradle to the grave?
Grieve! No welfare – just the state.
So can you please get your knees
off our fucking necks?

If all lives really matter,
why do some
so easily
get shattered?

Savannah Sevenzo
Silver Line

There is a silver line that divides the path
from the not path
in the part of St James's Park
that runs parallel with a red road
called Pall Mall.

I walk on it when I have nothing to think about.
It is just thinner than my smallest finger
it is perfectly straight.
I crush its parts with my big feet
for seconds at a time
the damage is never permanent.

The dust scuttles the path
blurs the divisions yet
when I lift my feet above the line
it is perfect and silver, intact beneath.
It testifies;
some parts of London are still 'untouched'.

I was born in London
though when people ask if I am a Londoner
the red-blue-white flags billowing at the side of Pall Mall
reply before I can;
their answer is negative.

Still, I have lived here long enough to wonder why
the Pall Mall road is red—
is it a stain?
Is it a decoration?
Are these things the same thing?
I only know
the red road is not mine.

Silver lines divide the *ours* from the *not ours*;
possessions from discoveries.
they keep my heart in its right place,
and my skin behind the glass.

Dipika Mummery
A Walk in the Countryside

Neetu retraced her steps for what felt like the fiftieth time, stalking down an unshaded country lane that looked much the same as every other lane she had come across since parking the car three hours earlier. She held her useless phone in one slippery hand, using the other to grip the thin, sweaty strap of her mini designer backpack. Her fringe stuck to her forehead and the neck of her t-shirt was uncomfortably damp. The lane was more of a rough track, and uneven stones poked at her feet through the thin rubber soles of her chafing canvas trainers. Neetu deeply regretted ever thinking that it would be a good idea to go for a walk in the countryside.

She had grown sick of spending her daily hour of outdoor exercise traipsing around Manchester city centre. None of her favourite stores were open, and the endless grey of tarmacked roads and featureless skyscrapers had become depressing. There were few green spaces near her flat. When the severe restrictions for Greater Manchester eased in July, Neetu decided that she was going to drive out to the countryside and see something different. She settled on leafy, affluent Cheshire after scrolling through the Instagram profile of an acquaintance, who seemed to have a wealth of countryside on her doorstep. She wouldn't get lost this time. She had downloaded a guide to the walk and Google Maps was on her phone. What could go wrong?

Everything, it turned out. Following the guide, Neetu had soon become confused by directions to turn left after a stile, that didn't seem to exist, and to turn right at a farmhouse that never materialised. She had opened Google Maps at that point but, contrary to what she had assumed, the app did not show every single country footpath.

Her signal was too patchy for her phone to consistently display a marker showing where she was. The only other people she saw were cyclists and drivers speeding past.

Ignoring the panic that threatened to overwhelm her, Neetu had decided to keep walking until she saw a landmark that signified civilisation. Surely there would be somewhere with a strong signal and a name that she could find on Google Maps?

She eventually reached the end of the lane and found herself at a familiar T-junction. She was pretty sure that she had gone left last time, so she went right instead. All she could see was hedges and blue sky. The heat shimmered from the baking tarmac, blurring her vision. Her tongue was painfully dry; she had drunk the last of her water ten minutes ago. The sun scorched the skin on her arms; the suncream she'd applied before she left the flat clearly hadn't been strong enough. This was heatwave weather.

She should have been lapping up the sun that shone so rarely in Britain and that she sought on luxury package holidays to Spain, Portugal, Italy and Croatia, not wandering around in circles in the middle of nowhere.

Despite herself, Neetu's mind leapt to a memory of a family holiday to India two decades earlier, when she had been eighteen. Her parents had always taken her to India in the school holidays to take advantage of the extended break from her studies, going for six weeks at a time. That last time, she had been gearing up to start university and study psychology. She had wanted to go to France with her friends, but her mother had insisted that she go to India instead. Visiting India in August meant a different kind of heat to the merciless heatwave sun here in Cheshire; humid, wet, energy-sapping. There would be the kind of heavy rain that thundered down for thirty seconds or thirty minutes at a time, hammering on the wonky roof of the buffaloes' shed by her grandparents' bungalow.

It was difficult not to think about arguing with her mother and standing under an alien tree, hoping that someone, anyone would come along and help her. She remembered all too acutely that terrifying feeling of being somewhere that she didn't recognise, with no way of getting back to what she knew. Her memories of the trips before that one were little more than a series of images, sounds and flavours – the lowing of a buffalo, the sun setting over rice fields, the smell of smoke from the kitchen fire, the creamy feeling of pistachio kulfi sliding over her tongue. She tried to focus on those sensations instead of conjuring up an old panic.

'I'd kill for an ice cream right now,' she said out loud, then caught a glimpse of a sheep staring at her through a break in the hedge. Unnerved by its steely glare, Neetu hurried on and wondered if she was suffering from heat stroke. How much longer could she keep going round and round in circles before she collapsed? And what if no one found her? She lived alone. She had told a friend of her plans for today, but what if she had wandered so far off the path that no one would think to look where she was?

Neetu shaded her eyes and peered towards the approaching end of the lane. Was that a roof? She sped up, ignoring the sweat that now dripped down the sides of her face, and was gratified to see a sign. A cafe. She would be able to buy a cold drink and shelter from the sun, and hopefully plot a way back to the car. The cafe would surely be on Google Maps.

Masked and sanitised, Neetu went in and bought a cold can of lemonade and a large bottle of water. Disappointingly, they were sold out of ice cream. She checked her phone as the teenager behind the counter served her. She saw that she had just enough signal to use Google Maps again. She hurried out with her loot, trying not to meet the eyes of the other customers. They were all white and much older than her. Pensioners with nothing better to do. She was used to entering spaces where there was no one else who looked like her, but it was still unnerving to be marked out as different by the stares of others.

Neetu stood in the shade of the cafe's awning and scrutinised the map. She realised with dismay that she had wandered much further from her intended route than she had thought. She would have to walk almost two miles to get back to the path, and then another mile from there to the car. She tried to memorise the route back, holding the cold can to her forehead with her other hand. Then she set off down the lane again, swigging her lemonade as she went.

The sun strengthened as the afternoon wore on. Neetu was grateful for the shade provided by tall overhanging trees as she left the rocky lanes that made her feet feel every twinge. She took a track snaking between a field and a forest. Freed from the worry of wondering where she was, she focused on her surroundings, finally revelling in being away from her flat and Manchester. Birds flitted past her and pecked at the ground before her, then disappeared up into the safety of the trees. She didn't have the first clue about identifying trees or birds, but she began to enjoy noting the differences between birdsong, feathers, beaks, bark and leaves. There was a neat abundance to the natural world here in the English countryside, a far cry from the person-sized leaves and grasses in the towering forest where she had got lost on that last trip to India.

Neetu's mind turned to the cafe and the watchful stares of the other customers, and the feeling of being somewhere she shouldn't. Was it because Indians never went for walks in the countryside here? She didn't know for sure, although she did know that immigrants like her parents tended to live in the big towns and cities where jobs were easy to come by, well away from the rolling hills and fields of the English countryside. In India, Neetu had never seen people going for strolls for the sake of it. Every journey seemed to have a purpose.

Of course, Neetu had gone on multiple holidays abroad since finishing her degree and moving to Manchester for work. She had travelled as far afield as Thailand and Vietnam, only giving India a cursory thought when the map on the in-flight entertainment screen showed her journey over the heart of the country. All of these holidays were to resorts, however. Self-contained oases of order and man-made structures. Well-signposted corridors and walkways. Efficiently organised tours with a defined start and end point. Neetu wouldn't know how to go about the sort of holiday that involved booking flights and accommodation, then organising meals and excursions and things to do, all while trying to navigate the streets and paths of a foreign location.

It was too loose. Too baggy with the potential for things to go wrong.

Like that last holiday in India. It had been a stupid argument. Unknown to Neetu, her mother had received enquiries from the families of bachelors in the village where her grandparents lived, all asking about Neetu. She hadn't realised what was happening until her mother took her to visit a family on the other side of the village. Both mothers quickly left Neetu and the man, who hadn't said a word, alone on the pretext that they were making tea in the kitchen. Neetu listened in vain for the sound of water running or of pans clanging. There was only a listening silence from behind the fringed curtain that separated the living room from the kitchen.

Later, Neetu had vented her anger at her mother. She had been harsh, but she had felt so righteous, so furious that her mother would try to divert Neetu from the path she had mapped out for herself – university, a high-paid job, independence, a few love affairs where she had the upper hand, maybe. Freedom. Look at you and Dad, she had said. Why would I want to be like you?

She had stormed off into the forest that fringed the village. A search party led by her father found her just before the sun started to fall from the sky. She was miserable and monsoon-sodden. Her mother wouldn't speak to her. Her grandparents stared at her in disapproval. For the rest of that holiday, she felt the whispers of the other villagers crowding her like gossiping ghosts. Relief had overwhelmed her when it was finally time to go home. Neetu hadn't wanted to return to India after that, and her parents stopped asking her to accompany them on their increasingly infrequent trips home. She got her degree, a job, regular holidays. Out of duty, she rang her parents once every two weeks, but they had nothing to say to each other.

Neetu remembered that she had meant to post photos of her walk online. She took out her phone and saw from the still-open map that she was now only half a mile away from the car. Where had the time gone? Her feet still ached, her skin was red and her whole being felt soggy with sweat, but she hadn't even thought about her physical discomfort in the last hour.

She took some photos of a tiny bird that alighted on a branch just ahead of her, and of a clutch of bright white flowers on the bushes at the side of the lane. Then the forest came to an abrupt end, and all she could see was sheep-dotted fields and the stark blue of the summer sky.

Neetu snapped some more pictures, then put her phone away with a shrug, not even bothering to memorise the rest of the route to the car. It was time to enjoy the view.

Shamini Sriskandarajah
My Sister's Care Home Promises

They stole my sister last November
And tried to pass her off as their own
With promises of a family Christmas
I'm still waiting for in March

No more her favourites *idiyappam* or *pittu*
Yellow *dosas* that she calls pancakes
But I shouldn't worry: they assure me
She has a McDonald's three times a week

I don't know if she remembers last year
And the thirty-something years before that
With her brown-skinned, black-haired sister,
An unpredictable glint in our golden eyes

Does she remember our grandmother's funeral
That I gazed at on my phone in silence
While she lay down and watched the cartoon
She had seen a dozen times before?

What colour are the Minions? I asked
As I took a selfie of us on her bed
Black, she said, while she stroked my hair
And ignored the yellow creatures on screen

They stole my sister last November
And tried to pass her off as their own
Cherry blossom buds begin to appear
And I'm still waiting for our family Christmas

Yvie Holder
Anchusa

It sent me back to your old books, which today
line my shelves. Spines that bored me as a child –
Common Weeds and *Plant Identification* –
drew me in, after a stroll round the village
this last day of May. Families wove
through lanes, stopped to ooh and aah at speedwell's
sky-drop deep in the verge, while cow parsley
laced shadows on the flush of children's cheeks.
It would have made you smile. I understand now,
Dad. Thirsty for facts, you'd have had this one
to hand, while I roamed around in dreams. *Weeds?*
you'd say, *jes plants growing in de wrong place.*
Today, I found *Anchusa, strong-rooted,*
thrives on margins, tough, gentian-blue. Perhaps
I'm in the right place and haven't lost you.

Anita Goveas
Baseline Measurements

Turtle Beach Residence, Abu Dhabi
Number of stars: ** Date of review: March 2019
Date of stay: Feb 2019
Title of review: It's been a long time since I ate a mango
Reviewer: Anonymous

I came across your guest house by stabbing my finger into a book of maps. Do you remember those? My Papa left one to me in his will, it's scented with secrecy and dried mango. I was expecting that, we used to read it every night when I was a child, plot point one of my journey to becoming a Geography teacher.

I didn't expect the letter he hand-wrote me, all shaky because the Parkinson's was winning at the end. The story of my father. I guess I'll find out how much of it is true.

I'd never flown before, never left London actually. I wasn't sure I could manage nine hours in a tin box, so I ended up here.

On the whole I liked it, it smells both of bleach and dust, something I didn't know was possible before. And the blind in the bathroom is held up by a paperclip, a true feat of engineering. I'm sorry I didn't go to the gym or the beach, but the water in the pool is beautifully blue. I enjoyed that the painted red rose on the bottom can only be seen from far above. I wonder how many guests have noticed.

Sorry, this is my first ever review, I hope some of it is helpful.

Field Marshal's Retreat, Hyderabad
Number of stars: * Date of review: March 2019
Date of stay: March 2019
Title of review: The distinctive smell of prawns
Reviewer: Nalini

I enjoyed the buffet breakfast, I ate three slices of mango and let the juice drip like honey over my lips and down my chin. And I've never been woken up by peacocks before, who knew they sounded like the love child of an angry baby and a machine gun? It's the fancy feathers they're known for, I'd never considered any other aspects of their beings or whether they had anything to make a noise about.

The main problem was I also woke up to the distinctive smell of prawns. Apparently, my father was allergic to prawns, but I am not. It was unsettling though. I couldn't tell where the smell was coming from, since I was facing the Gachibowli-Miyapur Road near the bookshop.

I guess, in the end, it didn't really matter, I was out most of the day.

Did you know the Institute of Surveying and Mapping is 52 years old? My father studied Geomatics there forty years ago, while my mother studied Pharmacy nearby. I made an appointment for a tour, but when I got there, I didn't go in. I'm already thinking of her every day now, what she would think of this trip, what she thought about leaving this place. She died when I was 14 months old, left me with a grumpy man who ignored me and a gentle grandfather steeped in secrets. But now I have to chance to get to know one parent, to try and make sense of all this information in the best way I know.

This is where they fell in love, but there's no grid reference that would show me where, no way to triangulate the start of this journey. I couldn't even find the prawns.

Classic Mansion Guesthouse, Jaipur
Number of stars: **** Date of review: March 2019
Date of stay: March 2019
Title of review: Pyaaz ki Kachori on the terrace (I think I've spelt that right) in the 'Pink City'
Reviewer: Nalini Chopra

I've never had anything so spicy for breakfast, it's great you have raitha and lassi for the tourists to wash away the sting. I'm not really a tourist, I was on a journey, it's very different. There's more plotting and researching involved. More considering the angles, more need for a baseline. Especially if the one you'd always relied on turned out to be false. I mean, even this city is redder than I was led to expect from the nickname.

I only really stayed here because my father grew up nearby, at least I know he lived near Bani Park for a while. There's a lot of five-star hotels and designer shops. And shopping malls. I wonder what this all looked like fifty years ago. I wonder if I walked anywhere he liked to go.

I'm tired now, I admit it. I've been travelling for a while, and nothing looks like Hampstead Heath, and I stayed up all night writing hotel reviews. I wanted somebody, somewhere to know where I'd been, to be able to follow my trail.

But the beds are soft here, and I got used to the chilies prickling on my tongue and the place I'm headed to might not want me. Maybe I'll be back.

Bird's Nest Motel, Chennai
Number of stars: *** Date of review: March 2019
Date of stay: March 2019
Title of review: Bombshells
Reviewer: Nalini Khan
Did you know the great trigonometrical survey of India

started near here? It took seventy years, sixty-five longer than they expected, I mean life just happens to you out of nowhere.

I think that's why my father wanted to be buried near here, I'm guessing, but I feel like I know him a little now. My real father, not the man I grew up with. I've been following a hand-drawn map, it fell out of a book that smells of mangoes and disappointment, and I don't think I was meant to have it. But maybe it was meant for me all along.

It had all these places crossed off on the back, Bani Park, the Institute of Surveying and Mapping, those places I did know about. They were in the letter as well you see, the letter that started this journey.

But the map is of Chennai, of my father's ancestral home, my home, I suppose, and I think there are people still living there. My family. They'd be able to tell me if I guessed right.

I'm going to knock on the door tomorrow, I'll be a bit of a bombshell, but I don't have anything or anyone to lose now. And if it goes well, I won't need another place to stay.

Rick Dove
Temporospatial Tongue Triangulations

Whipps Cross Hospital, Snaresbrook, August 2007
Always over mangos, these sticky shipyard street fights,
two great grandfathers clocking each other, across a divide,
Allies in ironically named Freetown, a port of Empire.

Later, both their future wives will love word games,
will die on the same day, but today, half a world away,
the half-sister of one, is on the wireless, as the sky falls over London.

Unlike time, flesh does not always dilate,
your old soul eyes, arrive newborn, and overdue (17 days),
landing on the second anniversary of the grandchildren, now
married.

Symmetry in overripe mangos, by the Hollow Pond we
circumnavigate
to get things underway. P, your nickname from embryonic days,
makes it onto the birth certificate, out of sheer relief,
as the Freetown Foursome celebrate,
hatchets long buried. A love of mango remains.

St George's Hospital, Tooting, August 1977
10 past 10 am, is 10 in binary. A deterministic ontology
in the symmetry of this arrival, from a galaxy not far away,
I Feel Love, by Donna Summer, is on the radio,
I know this, because later, it becomes a meme game.

It is a fabled, sultry, high summer, and after a long labour
mum's accent is still strong enough to undercut her white skin,
Mama Edwards' sang froid, an Ebonics jambalaya, hard dough
and Encona burning,
I know this, because forty years later, it still is,
its olive smooth cadence, in candour, no doubt stopped dead
loose lipped queries, about the 'darkie' in the buggy,
here in the town of Wolfie, a fist in the air in solidarity,
there is minimal NF graffiti, but still tension.

Later, a few miles away, jackboots will show defiance has
stubborn roots,
and I will play Chewie, not Lando, in the playground,
because his rage is more fitting, because I prefer not to speak,
because my tongue is still burning, because at 7, I know binary.

Lying In Hospital, Endell Street, St Giles, January 1902
That *we don't talk about it,* sounds like humility,
not the excommunication of a reality, that follows self-exploration
in defiance of patriarchy. This pioneer of the family,
this first black woman on the BBC, in the 1920s, found a voice
while not speaking.

Later, Google Doodles and an Ally Pally mural standing 20 feet,
a tribute to your voice, on the wireless, during our darkest hour,
but unlike the Forces' Sweetheart, you were swept
under a West African carpet, and the dissolution of Empire.

So it is circa 2013, in the National Portrait Gallery that first we meet,
me with a date, your headshot stops and captivates,
'you two have the same surname'
my voice becomes lost in the wireless broadcast, I am white
noise, shocked
to see my son in your eyes. For the first time, a face to a name.

Later, I will read poems about finding my place, existentialism,
and race,
in the building you were born in, now a private members' club,
'we don't talk about it' I will say, how London is in my blood,
and how, though we never discuss it, I love mangos, as much
as my son.

Sami Ibrahim
A Glossary of Terms

The words relating to the incident are as follows:
    Cold.
    Drowning.
    Funeral.
    Loss.
    Sadness.
Other words which relate include:
    Fear.
    Haemorrhaging.
    Instant.
    Struggle.
    Sleep.
Or perhaps:
    Dawn.
    Ice.
    Lake.
    Miscommunicate.
    Winter.
And then, finally, when I think about where I am now:
    Blame.
    Detachment.
    Error.
    Regret.
    Shock.
Twenty words is what she asked for. So that is what I have provided. All spider out from the central incident and all hold a certain weight on the page that I otherwise struggle to make

clear. When spoken, words tend to do one of two things. First, there are the words that become suddenly weightless. They dissolve into the air. Second, there are the words that are so heavy they sink through the floor. In both cases, I fear their meaning is lost on the moment of verbalisation and that starts another cycle of self-awareness and refusal. And when I'm paying this much for forty-five minutes, even she thinks it's a waste. This is why I've been asked to write instead of speak. Specifically write out lists. E-mail ahead and we can discuss in the session. Or use the session to write, if you'd prefer. Either way she was happy, she insisted.

Words I would use to describe the woman in front of me:

Caring.

Intelligent.

Older.

Thoughtful.

Warm.

Words I would use to describe what she sees when she looks at me:

Difficult.

Dull.

Reluctant.

Silent.

Twitching.

She laughs when she sees the latter, but the laughter is caring enough that I don't feel too small. Somehow, she makes it welcoming. She asks if I've ever considered who would be to blame and I tell her I haven't. This is patently a lie, and she knows it. She asks for a list of people who might be to blame:

Mike (maybe).

Mum.

Mum.

Mum.

Myself.

I also explain that unseasonably warm weather and the thinning of the lake's ice played no small part in things. She nods at this. She says that, in her eyes, thin ice would be the most likely culprit.

Books.

Exams.

Exercise.

Homework.

Maths.

These are the boring things. And then there's:

Dancing.

Kissing.

Music.

Sex.

Telly.

Which are the fun things. Although 'sex' is disingenuous for a young virgin – perhaps 'masturbation' would be more accurate. I don't bother to make the correction but from her raised eyebrows, it is obvious she knows. With hindsight, the boring list and the fun list seem to mould into one. But I have been asked for the list of things I don't do any longer and this is all I could come up with.

Words for Mum:

Annoying.

Lavender.

Loud.

Self-righteous.

Soup.

Words for Mike:

Annoying.

Chocolate.

Pushover.

Quiet.

Sweaty.

She asks if I have any positive words for either of them and I spend five minutes with the nib hovering above my notepad – before shrugging and saying no. When I say that perhaps *lavender* and *soup* are positive descriptions, she tells me that they are nouns.

If I could confront her now:

Crying.

Hitting.

Hugging.

Laughing.

Talking.

I would feel:

Anger.

Disappointment.

Fury.

Happiness.

Neglect.

And if I could speak to her, I would express it like this:

The limits of a list. But also, the limits of a sentence, because no sentence can be finely calibrated enough to contain the balance of hatred and forgiveness and relief that I would like to express in that moment. I tell her I'll never have to speak to Mum or Mike again so it doesn't matter. She tells me I might bump into them on the street. I tell her I'm far enough away that it won't happen. She tells me they might move closer. I tell her that Mum and Mike have, in their own words, 'already settled down'. And anyway, I don't get out much.

Abandon.

Boredom.
Confusion.
Panic.
Tranquillity.
Words are only words, she then tells me. Don't be intimidated by them because they mean as much or as little as we want them to. I tell her that's true. She tells me she doesn't believe I think that. I tell her I think it's true, apart from when the meaning of words are out of your control.

Go.
Outside.
Give.
Us.
Space.
Or when the meaning of words is in your control, but reality doesn't match up to perception.

The.
Ice.
Is.
Thick
Enough.
By this point, I am starting to wonder if the thing I should be blaming is the fragility of words, but that's such a stupid and abstract concept that I can't take it seriously. She smiles when I say this. She tells me that now I am starting to be in control.

Just.
Don't.
Be.
Too.
Stupid.
A command that I didn't obey. And another:

Back.
In.

Time.

For.

Tea.

At the burial, I was placed into the ground upright. It was an old church in Wiltshire, so Mum and Mike had to make a long trip from Norfolk. I am glad they did, because Dad was and is right next to me. And the family knew I wasn't quite ready to go, so they figured it would be easier for me to step out if I was already standing. The gravediggers weren't happy with the extra five feet of earth they had to remove, but when they saw how young I was, they conceded it was worth it. There was a month of waiting before I forced the courage to emerge. The murmuring voices above had long gone their separate ways and the ground was unfreezing. Dad whispered through the dirt: he told me I'd grow tired of the above world very quickly. He said I would start off wanting to confront people and lay things to rest, but it would soon dissipate. The young, especially, habituate quickly. And he was right. Partly. The world above is a terrible place when you've already left it. It is far too proud of all its life, and it overwhelms. Nevertheless, I have found that writing down words in the presence of a living human can be helpful.

Apologies.

Expectations.

Food.

Football.

Goodbyes.

A proper goodbye, she suggests, is what I am after. Shouting 'Back in time to tell you to fuck off' is not as effective a farewell as 'I love you, Mum'. This much is obvious, but sometimes the obvious is too large to comprehend. She asks for five more words. Reasons I have decided to seek out a therapist instead of making the journey to Norwich:

Cost.

Fear.

Inconvenience.

Pain.

Timetables.

And yet train tickets are not so expensive that I can't find the spare cash (they left money in my pocket in the hope I might return). And, she argues, the inconvenience is surely minimal given I have little else to do with my time. Other than that, the psychological reasons are simply things I need to come to terms with.

Except there are other reasons:

Decomposition.

Heat.

Smell.

Tiredness.

Ugliness.

She doesn't have such a good answer for that. Her pen shivers. She tells me it's a choice between shame and loneliness. Then she glances at the clock in a not-too-subtle signal. We decide to broach it all next time and leave things like this:

Awkward.

Hesitant.

Hopeful.

Plateau.

Stalemate.

When the session is over, I'm tired. We are scheduled in for next week, but I sleep for so long that the next time I step out, I discover that years have passed. Her office - just outside the centre of Salisbury - has moved. Gazing up at the building, I let people manoeuvre round me on the pavement. When the building's shadow disappears, around midday, I decide to leave. If she is not there to listen, then something else will have to do. I find that money has long since been devalued so the journey I purchase has to be one-way. It is hot and every time I notice other passengers sniffing at the stench, I move carriages to prevent further discomfort. With each move, I leave a patch of skin on the seat.

I have no doubt that Mum and Mike will still be there. After Dad went, Mum was so determined to settle that she glued her belongings to the new house's cheap laminate floor. Mike was unimpressed. Still, I often think that moving to Norwich was her way of stopping Dad from returning. And I often think that staying in Norwich is her way of allowing me to return.

The train pulls in and the walk out of the station unfolds like this:

Crowds.

Heat.

Nausea.

Nerves.

Traffic.

Which spews out such a thick smog I can't walk straight. Or maybe that's the nerves. Either way, the white lines on the road wriggle beneath the several-ton-weight of the cars. All the while, smog is still clagging my throat. It blurs my vision, pouring out of every vehicle, sitting in my long-failing eyes, and it is between the shifting forms of the smoke that I see:

Mum.

Too soon and too unexpected, because she is very suddenly right there. Weekly trip into town. Stood in the street. She drops her shopping when she sees me.

Apples.

Ketchup.

Love.

Soup.

Terror.

Mum.

She considers hugging, she considers not hugging, she stays still.

Breathe.

Frown.

Pause.

Smile.

Sweat.

Mum.

She asks me something, but I realise my ear is so damaged that I can't hear the words. She tries repeating herself, but it doesn't work.

Approach.

Comfort.

Cry.

Laugh.

Strain.

Mum.

Then she nods at me. It is as if she understands that her words won't be enough, they will never carry enough weight, so she wants to hear me speak. Sentences. Which I am completely prepared and unprepared for.

Blink.

Forgive.

Dry.

Gulp.

Swallow.

Mum.

Whose eyes hold me with patience. And it is in looking at her that I realise, finally, I have some words to say. Words that could be meaningful, words that could be healing or sensical or

Mum.

Mum.

Mum.

Mum.

Mum.
Mum.

Mallika Khan
A Man's Space

I used to try on my father's clothes.
His attire never seemed to fit me,
in his eyes anyway.
I felt the emptiness in his
work shirt,
envying how it compared to my shoes.
Leather and sole,
tightening its hold as if it were
pinning my feet to the floor.

My father could grow so tall
the roof would creak
as he leant his back against it.
I sucked in my stomach
but never protested. How could I
ask for more space than what he
had offered? He had gotten so big,
there was no room for my vocal cords.
So he ripped them out.

The pockets of air in his shirt
became a cold comfort.
Yet I wondered,
if I could stretch my skin
and blow up like a balloon,
could I fill a man's space too?
I could take my mother's hand,
tell her we need to leave.
Father takes up too much room now.

Growth has left little of me.
A pair of eyes
and a crooked tooth.
But my body still aches
to spread my arms
and fill my father's clothes.
To occupy a space he didn't
squeeze me into.
To stand beside not behind a man.

Someday I will no longer cower
before the men who forced their way
inside my skull
and scrubbed with soapy water.
Maybe I will learn that air
is a grateful reminder of my place
when I feel constricted.
That my space extends to the clouds;
and even further.

Alireza Abiz
The Dove's Throat

You crossed the Aegean on board a paper boat,
young Odysseus.
Rescue boats recovered you from water,
Lesbos wrapped you in Penelope's shroud.

Horses gallop in the desert.
Soft sand flows at dawn,
the sun rises like a sudden curse,
the song of a reed carries off the child of Balkh.

A viper's homesickness attacks me, attacks my dear soul.
I will catch it, place it in a bottle,
throw the bottle into this canal.
The wind will take the bottle to Fiji,
return it to the Gulf of Aden,
I will pluck it in bitter Konya.

Pour me a drink from the wine of this vineyard,
lay me down to sleep on cotton quilt clouds.
Pass me through barbed wire and concrete walls,
through rivers and seas,
forests and mountains.

How euphoric this port is!
Suddenly it rains nightingales.
I pass through the dove's throat,
alphabet letters in different languages scatter.

Bodies merge
limbs, eyes, gazes
souls and thoughts
move up, move down
to the left, to the right
forward, backward, to the future, to the past;
they approach and depart
and blend in the world's melting pot
to bake in time's oven like human dough.

A yellow flower has grown on the roadside,
darkness ascends through the valley,
lights appear beyond the border.

Balkh is the birthplace of the 13th Century Persian poet, Rumi,
in present-day Afghanistan

Seni Seneviratne
Without Borders

Millions on the move each year
crossing the peril of the Mediterranean.
Some get lost. Youngsters go astray.

Bad weather is bad news. Storms drive them
into the waves. Resting is risky: predators
have migrants on their menu.

They need safe havens, places to recover.
They fly towards the light but collision
with man-made structures can be deadly.

Some never finish the journey, exiled forever
in endangered spaces. Others settle and find
a welcome. We hear their amazing songs.

Mimi Yusuf
Journey to the Land Unknown

I leave my motherland
the journey is risky and long,
full of fear
that I am running from.
Comfort is a thing of the past
to go first is all I want,
into the high seas we sail
unaware of the dangers
we must hold what we treasure
life given by God
waves of the cruel sea speak to us
threatening to swallow us.

We sing songs of despair
praying to God that we reach
the promised land–
the hosts welcome us
assuring that all will be well.
That's not the case–
the wait is long
all hope departs.
All this time a question in my mind–
promised land, not sure,
motherland, not now,
where do I belong?

ZR Ghani
To Hope

To escape is to hope
                    defiantly–

I force a country into
                    my backpack
            in the rush

sleep for thousands of miles
                dreaming of the faces
I'll never see again

they melt away
                    in my efforts
            to tether their image

when we enter an empty room
my father calls home
                    my backpack slumps;

brewing under my brown
                    skin
                                is hope
                a seething sun
I used to know

When you have nothing to lose
but weeping
                        walls, a hole
by the window a two pound coin
                                can disappear
                into
and afford winter's long exhale,
the rats in the wardrobe
                        that chew
on school uniforms,
and scoff at un-British clothes,

when you can't shiver no more so you
                                convulse,

when they give you pictures
                        to read,
when years of rain purples your red coat,
all that remains is a dangerous smile
                                flashing
in the immeasurable distance,
and the treasured swarm
of feasting, shredding, torturous
                        hope.

Malka Al-Haddad
Yarl's Wood

I wrote a poem, two, three, ten.
I have not forgotten.

I swallowed all the spiders in my room,
lay on a hot oven tray,
drank all drainage in my shelter,
vomited everything I ate.
I have not forgotten.

Suicidal, sectioned, given 180 doses
to wash out my mind
in The Bradgate Mental Health Unit.
I did not forget.

Divided my life into pre-Yarl's Wood and
                                    post-Yarl's Wood,
bought the threads for my wedding dress,
sewed, embroidered, put it on, danced with my love.
I did not forget.

I shook hands with the sun on the shores of Wales,
felt tide and traction hundreds of times.
I have not forgotten.

Counted the stars in the sky of the Scottish Highlands,
the fields were green then parched ten times.
I have not forgotten.

Hung my memories on a washing line,
waited for them to dry, and went back to say: Yarl's Wood
is not forgotten.

This morning I looked in the mirror at my white hair
and realised I have got older faster than I could imagine.
I will never forget.

*Yarl's Wood Immigration Removal Centre is a detention centre
for foreign nationals before their deportation from the UK,
a form of kidnapping and psychological torture.*

Seni Seneviratne
Triptychs from the Hungarian Border

1.   For a three year old

she crawls	she's through	her dad crawls
under razor wire	hands moving	inching
palms flat	forwards	away from danger
on the ground	body	under razor wire
one coil inches	raised	held high
from her hair	her head	by men he trusts
her dad knows	with brown curls	she stands tall and
she must stay	determined	smiling
grounded	proud	arms akimbo
keep watch	with courage	her eyes looking
from right to left	in her next steps	to the future

2.   For a six month old
Don't be afraid my child, look I'm here waiting for you.
Soon, soon you'll be with me but don't touch the fence
that razor wire draped in coils could cut your baby fingers.

Don't be afraid darling, feel how your uncle's open palm
has made a seat to steady you, holding you up like an offering.
Can you see that clever man balancing above your head?
That's your daddy, walking a tightrope of metal? Don't worry,
he has hold of your arm. I know it feels too tight, my love
but he needs to lift you. I know two hands feel safer
but one of his hands needs to hold back the wire's blades
to clear a gap, big enough for your precious body.
Soon, very soon, my baby, you'll be in my arms again.

Don't be afraid, little one, you were born under bombs
and see how you've survived. We are looking beyond
these cruel fences, for some kind 'hellos', a place to settle.

3.   For a nine year old

I watch	I wait	I move
hands lift	for my turn	slowly
sharp blades	wonder if	slither
pull my fleece	the threads	under
my hood	will snag	a gap
down over	my jeans	feel dirt
my fringe	embroidered	scratch
think of	roses	my palms
tangled	carefully	then up
hair	sliding	dancing
another girl	through	success

*In 2016, Hungary built a more than 100-mile-long razor-wire border fence
to keep fleeing refugees from Syria out of the country.*

Marina Sánchez
They Call Themselves
Las Águilas del Desierto/ The Eagles of the Desert
'There is no choice but to cross the desert. The journey is not two days but five, six,
seven or ten. Once they get in, they cannot return'.

Las Águilas del Desierto swoop down
                    once a month, hiking for hours
         in the desert heat
              among volcanic rocks, snakes and
saguaro cacti that seem to hold up the sky.
        The smell on the breeze is their compass and map.
 They poke sticks under bushes
              climb up and down ditches
dotted with clothing, rosary beads and
           discarded water bottles painted black.
Then the whistle blows and radios crackle
      Encontrámos un cadáver/We found a corpse.
Under the shade of a small tree, a man, still fully fleshed.
        A cloud of flies above his swollen chest
pus and blood leak from his mouth.
              Recent. An unusual find.
The desert heat can strip a body to its bones in weeks.

      Then the ritual:
           tape off the area
           radio coordinates to Border Patrol
           pray for the dead man's soul
           lay a cross next to his body.

After a skull, he is the second find that day.

        Once they found eleven sets of remains.
Another, they found nine bodies huddled in a line.

        The *Águilas* have also crossed, lost relatives.
The worst is lack of water

        then broken bones from walking at night
and coyotes, vultures, rattlers.

        'When I find the remains of migrants, they are me.
If it wasn't us, who would find them?'

Found poem from a CNN article

Ambrose Musiyiwa
Rollercoasters

rollercoasters
have many layouts
many heights
many types
many effects

after some rides
you walk away
like you just got off
a park bench

others
need you
to take time
find yourself
gather
test the ground
see if you can leave

Dean Atta
Translate This Sentence

'Η οικογένεια μου είναι
πολύ μακριά από εδώ.'

'My family are
very far away from here.'

Another correct solution:
'My family is
very far away from here.'

Whether 'is' or 'are',
my family are far,

and learning Greek
does not bring them
closer to me right now.

I cannot comprehend
this situation but I can focus
my attention εδώ. Here.

Lesley Kerr
The Way Back Home

Grace sank back gratefully into the air-conditioned taxi, the heat and noise of Port of Spain's Piarco International Airport fading into the distance – taking with it any lingering doubts.

Her three children initially had concerns about her leaving the UK, where she had made her home for more than forty years, unaware that she and their father had planned this for many years. After a while her sons, who were both busy with careers, wives and families, became more encouraging, as her determination and anticipation became apparent. Her daughter Lydia however, remained sceptical, repeating stories of people she had heard of who had retired back home only to drop dead a few months later, or couples who divorced due to the husband slipping easily into the old life of 'liming' with friends, or playing dominoes while the wife was expected to occupy herself at home.

However, Grace held firm. Once the shock of her decision had passed, the children supported her, surprised that their parents had saved sufficient money to not only buy her childhood home, but also to supplement her pension. In the end, it was Lydia who had helped with the arrangements, completing the mountains of paperwork involved in tying up one life and starting another.

Grace thought fondly of Errol and her resolve grew stronger.

She thought, too, of her siblings who had been flung in different directions across the globe. Her brother to Toronto, her big sister Gwen to New York, and then Atlanta. She herself had ended up training as a nurse in a cold, unfriendly, country ravaged by war.

This was the first time Grace had returned to Trinidad since she had left all those years ago – mindful of her mother's instruction to make a life for herself in the Motherland.

Work hard, keep your head down and don't come back, she had said to her youngest daughter, aware of the limited options available in their small town. Grace knew that her mother had her best interests at heart, and when Mama had months left to live, she had moved to Toronto to be cared for by Grace's brother, determined that Grace would not come back to Trinidad.

Grace listened absently to Neville's chatter as the taxi navigated the dusty roads, and was comforted by his familiar patois. Her own accent had long since been diluted – only re-emerging during telephone conversations to friends or family back home; when she would be teased about sounding 'More English than de Queen!' Over the years the telephone calls turned to talk of where other friends and family had moved to, as more and more people left her small town.

'Yuh see, dis is where the print mill was,' Neville gestured cutting into her thoughts, 'yuh remember?'

Grace nodded her head.

'Is a university now,' he continued. 'How long yuh been gone?'

'Long time,' she answered.

'Back from H'england, eh?' He shook his head. 'Lots been coming back, yuh know, and not just from de Windrush…'

Grace nodded again. She had never felt that England was her home, despite raising a family there and giving more than forty years' service to the NHS. In the early years of working in hospitals, patients would hiss at her: 'I don't want your dirty black hands on me!' Grace would always reply stoically, 'Well, I'm the only nurse here, so it's me, or nothing.'

Her mother's often repeated phrase, that she would have to work twice as hard to get half as far as the UK-born nurses, was sadly prescient, and it was a message she passed on to her own children.

She had met Errol when he was working as a technician at the American airbase on the island. Her mama was grateful that she had not brought home 'One of dem damn Yankee soldiers', who had a reputation for leaving the local girls either heartbroken or pregnant when they moved on.

Errol left for the UK before Grace and the early years had been hard for him too. His qualification in engineering was deemed worthless, but he found employment as a driver on the London Underground, initially working the graveyard shift, along with other immigrants who had to prove their worth before they were put on the same rotas as the English men; but the times had slowly changed, and life was easier for her children and grandchildren. Her boys had mostly stayed out of trouble, and now had good jobs and large families, while Lydia became the first in the family to go to university; but the bitter taste of those early years lingered.

Like many Caribbean nurses, Grace was trained as an inferior State Enrolled Nurse, unlike her English counterparts, training for the State Registered Nurse programme. She had worked with prejudiced ward sisters who assigned the Caribbean nurses the most demeaning tasks, such as assisting the untrained auxiliary nurses with feeding or cleaning the ward, instead of being treated as a qualified nurse. The ward sisters would insinuate that she should be glad of the opportunity for this work – even dirty work, until such time as she proved herself.

Grace became used to doctors dismissing her voice in handover meetings because of her accent, but still, she worked tirelessly to prove them wrong.

When Lydia went to secondary school, Grace decided to do the conversion training to become a State Registered Nurse, despite opposition from Errol, who did not see the need for her to better herself as he had started to earn more, and the family had become comfortable. He tired of Grace's need to always 'prove yourself to them people', saying that 'no matter how hard we work, we will always be outsiders'. Deep down, however, he knew how important it was to her to fulfil her potential; it was this intelligence and determination that he loved about her.

She had risen through the ranks, becoming a senior sister, ward manager and finally, lead nurse for the Trust's geriatric services until her retirement.

The taxi lumbered farther into the countryside and Grace relaxed as the streets became those of her youth. She recognised the familiar shuttered windows and porches on the houses that provided respite from the unforgiving sun. On the sidewalks the fire hydrants stood sweating in the heat.

'This you?' Neville stopped the cab outside the small house. The freshly painted porch and newly cut lawn provided a welcome sight.

'Yes, this is us,' Grace replied.

Neville left the cases on the porch and said, 'Welcome home, we'll see you around – is a small place!'

Grace smiled gratefully and stepped into the cool of the house. She was thankful that she had let her granddaughter set up a delivery with a local shop in Tunapuna, who remembered the family, and organised the extravagance of a housekeeper, who had put the groceries away along with opening and airing the house.

Grace moved through the reception rooms, barely believing that she was back in her family home. The sounds of laughter and music, and long forgotten memories echoed in her head, seeming to bounce off the walls.

She glanced down at the dining table to see a note from the housekeeper propped up against a loaf of fresh sweetbread and guava fruit wrapped in wax paper. Her eyes pricked with tears as she read.

Welcome home Grace!

I trust you had a pleasant journey. The cupboards are filled, and you will find everything you need for the next few days, but if there is anything you need, please call me no matter the time. We are looking forward to seeing you at Church on Sunday, you will find it much changed on the outside, but I know you have been with us online over the last few years. The Pastor's wife, Gail, has arranged a lift for you, and lunch after the service, where you can meet some of our members.

The ladies' group meets on Tuesday evenings, and I have taken the opportunity to include you, and can arrange to take you if you wish.

Welcome again, dear Grace, and many good wishes for this new chapter in your life.

Madeleine.

Grace folded the note as tiredness mixed with relief washed over her. She picked up the fruit, and walked into the back yard, savouring the scent of hibiscus in the air.

Placing a small urn carefully onto the tiny patio table, she said, 'There, Errol, we finally come home.'

Dean Atta
Haibun for your return

The gate creaks open, in need of oil. Your footsteps on the gravel. The padlocks on the bike shed click open. Next, will it be your pannier removed from the side of your bike or your helmet placed on the roof of the shed, will it be your bike tucked in next to mine, will you remember to remove the water bottle from your bike or lock it in the shed for the night, will you ask to drink from mine at bed time? Shed locked, gravelly footsteps, creaking gate, then you're at the door, as usual, you try the handle before putting your key in, as if I would have left it unlocked all day. Perhaps I should have unlocked it for you.

> Because, after all,
> you announced your arrival
> with so many sounds.

Sundra Lawrence
Summer '95

Returning from a movie in downtown Colombo
our family are stopped by armed police at a checkpoint.
It is late and we are Tamil. Singhalese officers poke a flashlight
into the back of the tuk-tuk; blanch faces in dusk.

The driver keeps his hands on the wheel, tries to open
a conversation. A peaked cap officer questions my mum:
Where are you going? Where have you come from?
She answers in rusty Singhalese arpeggios.

ID! Mum pulls from her handbag a batch of burgundy passports,
places them on top of her oversized black one,
gold letters of *United Kingdom* flare.
The officer opens the Sri Lankan passport first; his torch

picks out the shiny photo and English
name. Place of Birth: Valaan, Jafna. Silence.
He thumbs the pages of our passports like a royal
flush, but stops at my brother's childlike shot.

Now fifteen, his faint moustache seems thicker in this light.
They tell him to step out. Mum pleads, *but we are British.*
I want to shame them with my London vowels.
The officer tells the driver to turn off the engine –

for us to wait in the vehicle. We understand the metal
instruction of rifles. The men encircle my brother;
his shoulders are casual, dark denim,
collar up, like he's hanging with his mates.

Our driver pelts the steering with his fingers
like type-bars, striking a letter of complaint.
Mum pinches each stone of her rosary,
glass beads scratch fast prayer.

My breath is somewhere in the polythene seats.
The officer returns, tips up his cap, rubs the bald crease
above his frown, then asks Mum where she grew up.
Mutawal, Colombo. The surprise unhooks his scowl.

Mutawal, he repeats, his mouth relaxes
on each syllable. *That's where I'm from.* His voice
is song; stories of neighbourhood, and when did she leave?
The passports and my brother are returned.

Please, go straight back to your home.
He slaps the stretched tarp above us.
The gas pedal goes down, the engine climbs
in pitch, like a nest of wasps nearing.

*The Sri Lankan Civil War (1983-2009) raged between minority Tamils and majority
Singhalese. Amnesty International reported on the number of Tamil boys and young men
taken and tortured for information about the LTTE, their bodies dumped on roadsides
or never found.*

Kavita A. Jindal
Cocoon Lucky

It is December and I dwell on what fortune-tellers have told me in the past. There is not much else to do when 'festive season' occurs while we're in lockdown. I'm semi-shielding, actually. Everything I do is half-baked and prefixed by semi or demi. Nothing is full-on, not even make-up for work Zoom calls or Zoom parties. Lipstick and a pearl pin in my unruly hair is enough, isn't it?

I am trying to decide if I feel the need to go out or not. I'm quite content within my walls. I'm quite comfortable, thank you. I do like having walls.

The soothsayers of my past had a hit rate of fifty percent in their predictions, which is what you'd expect. Some of them had rare imaginative detail, and it is that detail that made their predictions striking when it turned out something they said would happen, happened. One of them said I'd die abroad. I won't be able to comment on that one when it happens. Anyway, what is abroad?

Last year included travel to a beach. Last year in December there were festive happenings. I went along to a few Christmas drinks parties, but, one year on, they are hazy in my memory. I recall just one vividly. I remember walking into a buzzing room, getting entangled in my own coat as I attempted to hand it to the daughter of my friend, who was on coat duty, and accepting a glass of fizz from my friend's son, who was on drinks duty.

*

A knot of people are in intense conversation, and I join them

110

because I know two of the six, so I can say 'Hello', and they can expand out to make space for me. I have inadvertently fallen into a serious discussion about passports. After Brexit you know, they want to be sure that they, and their kids, also have European passports, so that they can access Europe as Europeans – as well as being British, of course. Some of them were born in other European countries. Others have heritage. I am used to this; I have friends who are now also nationals of Ireland or Portugal, because one of their parents was born in those countries.

One of the men in the group is grumbling about how very long his new naturalisation process is taking. 'This is so important,' he says, 'and it's taking months. Months. My country can do better. It's the European leader in technology.'

'It's not,' another man cuts in. 'Finland is the nerdiest country in Europe. My country.'

'Aren't you American?' I ask.

He smirks. 'That's one of my passports. But I need a European passport now. This whole Brexit thing is so ridiculous.' Six people nod sympathetically at him. They all need a third or fourth passport for their children. Being British as well as non-EU nationalities is not enough, now, we need European papers too, for free movement.

I am possibly more sick of this talk than all of them, but that's because I find a passport a strange thing.

True identification of individuals is good, we need that for society and security. But to predicate movement on which passport one holds? When a passport can be the same as an accident of birth. One day we will have a different system.

I am tempted to talk about the refugees they have little sympathy for. Refugees are escaping something, hardship, at the very least, if not terror, and if they had the means they would waltz into Britain and buy citizenship like the planet's criminals do. One passport would do them. One right kind of passport. I don't say anything because we are at a party, and two of them know my schtick anyway.

The others may have guessed my thoughts from the curl of my lip. One of them hard-nudges my arm in a friendly gesture, almost tipping my wine. 'Of course, these are first world problems,' she laughs.

I don't want to curb their discussion with my sniffy expression.

'I can't contribute much here,' I say, 'so please excuse me.'

I make my way to a white sofa and sit on it, attempting to affix a more pleasant half-smile on my face.

'Let's not be judgmental,' I say to myself. I know these are all lovely people. They are doing what they can to continue to prosper. They don't want any country that they live in to be overrun by the world's poor, that's all. And if they happen to belong (in mind, body and passport) to three countries, why then, they don't want the world's poor to overrun any of those nations. Sometimes I have asked them if some of those refugees might perhaps contribute more to the country they come to, than some of the 'born here' folks. Not that these people were 'born here', but as people with good fortune, it is different for them. They are always 'legal', aren't they? I ask, sometimes, who provides all the things they love, such as dining out and embroidered garments? Who will provide the vaccine when it comes? Will it be former refugees, will it be 'foreigners'? Ah, I can be quite boring.

I can also be envious. Because I would've liked to have kept a passport that I had, oh, twenty-five years ago, but that country didn't allow dual citizenship. So, I'm a one-citizenship gal.

I hope my half-smile is making me look pleasant and not a crosspatch.

It is Christmas and anger has no place in seasonal cheer. Nostalgia is permitted. Surfacing sorrows are allowed to zipline, everyone talks about losses at Christmas. An annual accounting that turns into a profit-and-loss table of years past.

I too, have affection for at least three countries, and heritage I can call on, but to gain one kind of freedom, I had to give up a part of me. You could say obtaining freedom of movement cost me the trusting part of my soul. I am suspicious of human beings the world over. I talk to animals, mostly the domesticated or urban types.

I do talk to human beings. All I'm saying is I can be changeable. I can be the life of the party, but not this one. That first conversation I entered has plunged me into a soup of mixed emotions. Should I speak up? For the world? To the world? No, sit tight, sit quiet, love the life I have, don't complicate fragile comradeships.

The family's dog, a chocolate-brown labradoodle, who knows about unconditional relationships, sashays to the sofa to nuzzle me. 'Oh, you've found me,' I say. Its tail wags, and its eyes are alight with recognition. I'm the lady who dispenses long strokes. This is such a photogenic animal. It has posed so beautifully for the family greetings card. Last year the dog even sent its own Christmas card in addition to the family's one. It was signed. This is a dog with good handwriting, and I am on the favoured list.

I mutter up my gratitude to the universe for friends who offer good wine, classy canapés and a good-looking dog who acts as my sofa sentry, adding to my aura. I should be so lucky.

*

This Christmas I am counting my walls and feeling cocooned. My walls are painted 'deep slaked-lime' chosen from an environmentally friendly paint colour chart. I'm offering myself my own good wine and eating 'starters' from my grocery shop. These duck spring rolls apparently serve four people, but do me nicely as a meal for one. After a bit of clearing up I just have to toddle to bed and read my book.

Or I could answer my three hundred pending emails.

Or I could go for a walk.

I have been resisting evening walks this December. A strange inertia. Last year I walked home from that Christmas party that I remember so well. I even recall the walk home.

*

My neck is bundled in a red wool scarf. I've barely taken a few steps when a black cat detaches itself from the dark spaces by a fence and shimmies alongside me. 'At least you're not crossing my path,' I speak aloud to the cat, and it doesn't run away. 'You're just bored and coming along for the walk home, looks like.'

All these superstitions about black cats – some good, some bad. What I believe depends on my temperament at the moment. Tonight, the cat is a good omen. In truth, a cat, black or not, is good. I have not yet found myself in a mood where I mind a cat crossing.

The cat meows and slinks so close to my legs that I can feel it. In a few minutes I will be home. The new LED street lamps are so white and bright. A fox crosses my path. It pauses to note my glance, and darts into darkness, into someone's garden or the children's playground.

'Alright.' I'm speaking to steady myself. There are good and bad superstitions about foxes crossing a person's path. Like with the cat, I usually take a fox as a good omen. It is living, it is doing its city thing. When I was young, my grandmother used to let me dress up in her fox pelt stole, complete with fox's head. I have to say I loved it then. That was the first fox I had seen – a dead preserved one. Now I regularly spot my local foxes, sometimes snoozing in the sun on the top of my neighbour's shed. Sometimes they startle me at night, like this one, that has crossed my path with a message, perhaps, and disappeared.

I realise I have stopped, and so has the cat. I walk on and turn into my front door. 'Coming in?' I ask the cat. I go in and turn on the lights in the hall. The cat prowls around the front of the house, it has found something to interest it. I say goodnight and close the door on my harbinger of luck, hoping it sticks around. I already have some luck, that I have clawed for and clawed at over the years, but I can do with more. Who couldn't? When luck was a no-show I went about my business determined to greet it with open arms when it came. For many people it may feel like it never shows up at all, despite all the graft they put in. And in some life-stories, you do feel that ill luck has dominated.

It's hard to know if anyone else is as silly as I am, believing minute encounters to be visitations of luck. But believing in a universe that listens to my muttering is good for me, it allays the tedium of the perpetual striving that is life.

*

This Christmas season I'm finding excuses not to walk in the evening. Semi-shielding can be tiring. Just the constant deciding what not to do and what to do, organising enough food for the end-of-the-world (although will I be here to eat it?), and keeping up with what is allowed or when it will be allowed. My bubble-person is also semi-shielding, which makes two of us in a semi/demi state. In my holding pattern, I just wave to the neighbour's cat through the window. It sits on my sill, outside, its eyes flashing when they catch the light.

This December, I count my walls. I can eat in one room and work in another. I can sleep.

This December, in my dreams I am bounding about like a maniac at different latitudes and longitudes across the globe.

Friends who are dead come to speak to me. My body lies tranquilly through this hectic adventuring. My body enjoys its familiar comforts, even in semi/demi state. It likes to be parked in its cocoon at home.

Home is where I have walls of my own to count. Anywhere else is abroad.

Sandra Nimako-Boatey
A place to call

I think of how thrilling it would be to live alone.
The freedom.
The solitude.

But then I remember I am an unhinged thing.
I'd stay up drinking and smoking until 3am,
thinking myself into despair.

At home I am rooted.
Let me go and unshackle me and I am afraid that I might
                                                    just crumble.

Run my hands along a sofa that is mine.
A throw that is mine.
Sink my feet into a rug that is mine.
And sink my teeth into my forearm to stop me crying out.

I will be without chains
and I feel I may come tumbling down.

Marka Rifat
My Fault

I thought I lived in Scotland but learned
from pages worn soft by generations
of little fingers
that my young feet
walked in the low lands, called Uplands,
while in grainy black and white,
there were bounded Great Highlands
further north than I could imagine.

Worryingly, both
were faulty.

But we had a famous crag and tail behind our council house
and igneous islands in the Forth
and a basalt throne on the East Bay sands.
Surely treasure enough and tangible.

In middle age, I saw the fabled Boundary land
and smiled that those glowing Lothian fields
of childhood were the Old Red Sandstone echoes
of the sunset soil
and now I glory to walk in minutes
to the mythic point, where I had laid
a wooden ruler to test my teacher's claim.

I sit with seals at Garron Point
as vast North Sea waves
strike and scour the soft
and slide defeated from the rest:
my textbook fault.

But can I believe
that the rock I touch
with blue fingertips
can be seen from space?

Rachael Li Ming Chong
Hi-Spy Viewing Machine

The ocean zoomed in
seven times
looks exactly like the ocean you
lament
roving your hire eyes
for signs of an earth
where banana leaves
substitute surfboards
jellyfish pitch into four-man tents
the crest of a wave can be sugared
then shaped
with sand buckets
a cake
for your neighbour's
wedding
I spun it one-eighty once
to see your laughter echoing off the brow
of the Japanese Alps

Never Let Me Go rolled
in your back pocket

final page
anaemic
from re-reading
you'd been
riding funiculars
towards the break of the sun

don't get me   wrong

there   too
were signs   of weathering
pockets padded   with last year's receipts
and rubbed-worn   totems
though that was when
the soil of your tread
vibrated   urgently
to breed planets
when hope

was handwoven
when the ocean
zoomed in

seven times
exactly
did not look like
the ocean

Yvie Holder
East Coast

These waters where I've played in the shiver of waves;
where I've swung our children over sands – one two three
four five six weeeeee! – and picnicked late in the chill,
soothing burnt skin and salt-stung eyes

these waters, same waters

that my grandfather, Christopher, cycled to check
on Trinidad's dirt roads, from tropical sun-up
to its evening glow, measuring the stand-pipes' flow,
its clarity, as Chief Turncock for the colony; angered
to see a wasted drop; pushing daily past Queen's Park,
glad of a stop under the Samaan's
deepest shade;

these waters, same waters

that seeped down hills green and red with immortelles
and bamboo, beneath the cocoa-palms' wide sway,
to where, beside her chickens and goats, his wife,
Robertha, bathed each of their children, the ten
who mewled and fed, and the one two three four five six
dead at birth

these waters, same waters

that before her, dripped crosses on foreheads
of babes at a font on a Barbados plantation; that
before them, eased the raw throat of Francis
and the lashed skin of his mother, Bellah,
her eyes salt-stung
before him

was it these waters, these same waters

that carried you, dear ancestors, to those lands

and brought me to these sands

and to you?

Oluwaseun Olayiwola
SE16

Watch:
Playground in the cemetery.
When it snows children use the headstones
as the bottoms of snowmen–

Sky dissipating its frigid blossoms over the balconies, the square
couples, back-lit, holding each other like witnesses –

At their windows

everyone forgets the sun exists altogether, all together.

Off and on and off
the infrared light of the body goes–disappointing.
What heat lingers? the children's

hands reaching, like tattered kites,
to catch a snowflake in their rose-coloured palms;
the higher meaning of transformation: unclear,

the snowflake burning like ice in their palms.

Now, it is rain. now
the playground is an everywhere–
So many dead, so many grieving.

Their mothers take their faces
in cold hands, wash them again
and again like a stain in a glove–

snowing harder now
life goes on this way
a white sheet

covering
us all

PA Bitez
Ife

you become lovesick with stars
every time the heavens take hold of your heart;
i can see the marrow in your bones foam
when you start to think of the Obatala's art,
the way he built us with Olorun's single breath,
crafted our bodies from a blank canvas

instead of a rib, gave us a whole language
that is woven into the seams of our lips.
do not let the salt in your mouth make you any less tender; do
not let despair become your water,
the rain in your eyes, the wars in the tips of your fingers, the
four oceans found in the brief flood of a smile.

it is always summer in our skin; the sun is painted all over it.
do not believe them when they say love is only for winter
women,
Osun did not agree to rebirth just to leave you lonely,
remember our wombs are the first glimpses of heaven
our children will ever see, our bones, our blood,
our births, the first gifts to this earth.

our muscles will tell the story of metamorphosis;
how the climate of our skin had to change for colder countries.
i am so sorry they made you eat your own mouth,
how skin the colour of coal was not allowed,
how your flesh became raw with rejection and renown,

how you learned to endure your name being mispronounced,
how the mispronunciations became your name.
now you burst into dreams even when awake.
do not let yourself become a lost language,
your body was never meant to become a debate.

homeland in your hands, left oceans and sands
for gravel and pavement. watch the sun stop
to stare at you, a stunning walking miracle
so divine that they made you mythical,
scribed fables and called it truth to defame
love's personhood.

Alexander Williams
Yarmouk University

The Boys

Here are real men
Boys once, fleetingly, eternally
Ready and eager to grow,
Rounding out like tree trunks
Arms brown as sturdy boughs.

The specimens in Europe
Pale in comparison
Mere waifs and paltry strays
With no hair upon their chests.

Here their strength is visible,
Flaunted ostentatiously:
Bulging sun-bronzed biceps
Oiled with sweat
Rich bark-brown skin
Darkly shining in the yellow air
T-shirts tight as vests
Jeans like body paint.

They hold hands like brothers
Or lovers, linking arms,
Lying one on top of another
Like blankets on grass
Leaning back to shoulder
With masculine ease
And feminine affection.
Skin rubs and fingers intertwine
And never does a local eyebrow lift,
Though mine rise quickly heavenward.

Here the males are unafraid to touch,
Intimacy is boyish, vanity manly
As they admire themselves
In the mirror of each other.

Victoria Ekpo
Yoga with the Black Mothers Group

I'm not a mother and no longer plan to be,
Not one borne of my womb anyway.
But I am a woman all of the time
And one in desperate need of a yoga class which:
    Isn't in my gym,
    Isn't where my butt sticks up the highest in the downward dog,
    Nor where the teacher is too 'zen' to correct my pose.

The teacher was late, class started late,
But the long time, how dos
Keep us company as much as the late evening sun.
Mats down and we salute said sun,
At the downward dogs, all the butts stick out high – normal.

    My boobs pop out at forward fold,
    A wink directs me to similar plopping bits.
    The lines drawn on their bellies resemble mine,
    Our tones mixed from a pot stirred from different hearths
                        – so, never mind.

    The happy baby pose signals a drawing close in giggles,
    Of wobbles and jiggles and groans,
    I smile and feel my heart contract
    For I have found my yoga home at last.

Nasim Rebecca Asl
Yalda 1400

We sat, cross-legged, read Hafez and told each other
our futures. I asked my question first, muted syllables crouched

on my tongue. Let you flip the pages. Left my fate
in your hands. Eyes scrunched tight, you stopped

the divan – Ghazal 112. Pomegranate juice jewelled your lips
as you told me, this year, I should spend more time in nature:

Sit by a river once a week, at least. Let the tides marinate your thoughts.
Your tongue is too rusted to make out the rest so you pass

the book to me. I map your year for you: Ghazal 140. Heartbreak.
Someone will hurt you. You'll be a doe whose fawn is crumpled on the curb

a wolf rejected by its pack, a swan incubating eggs that never hatch.
I apologised for bearing bad news, but Hafez said it, so it must
be true.

You laughed. The lifelines of your hands, palms sticky with
watermelon,
reached for mine. I held your fingers as we solsticed into winter.

About Arachne Press

Arachne Press is a micro publisher of (award-winning!) short story and poetry anthologies and collections, novels including a Carnegie Medal nominated young adult novel, and a photographic portrait collection.

We are expanding our range all the time, but the short form is our first love. We keep fiction and poetry live, through readings, festivals (in particular our Solstice Shorts Festival), workshops, exhibitions and all things to do with writing.

https://arachnepress.com/

Follow us on Twitter:
@ArachnePress
@SolShorts

Like us on Facebook:
ArachnePress
SolsticeShorts2014

Where We Find Ourselves is the first in a series of anthologies loosely linked by the theme of Maps and Mapping.

Coming soon:

What Meets the Eye, the Deaf Perspective, Nov 2021

Words from the Brink, Solstice Shorts 2021, Climate Crisis, Dec 2021

and

A470, Bilingual Poems for the Road, Mar 2022 (Welsh & English.)

Find out more about our authors at
https://arachnepress.com/writers/